Serendipitously, this manuscript was sent to the publisher on

World Sparrow Day

March 20, 2022

Heart Of The Sparrow

Stories of my Life

Erika Mannheim Schafer

For my dear
friend Clé
Thank you for over
40 years of
sharing and caring.
Love
Liz
August 2022

3

For permission requests, write to the author, addressed "Heart of the Sparrow: Permissions" at erika.denver@gmail.com

Ordering Information:

For details, contact erika.denver@gmail.com

Print ISBN: 978-1-66784-586-9

Printed in the United States of America on SFI Certified paper.

First Edition

Sparrows are symbolic of living a meaningful and peaceful life. They bring confidence to you and make you believe you can achieve whatever you wish for.

Worldbirds.com

For Birgit and Heidi

I dedicate these pages to the
loving memory of
my parents

Wilhelm and Elfriede Mannheim

Contents

Prologue   13

Introduction   15

Growing Up In Düsseldorf   17

My Parents   18

My Grandparents   31

Ode To Mutti   36

Howeweg 1 - Our Home   41

Child Of War   45

Foreword   46

War Memories   48

The Escape   56

Rebuilding After The War   58

A Thing Of Beauty   67

After The War   70

Foreword   72

About Money   73

Christmas At Home   76

How We Met   82

Music In My Life   86

Message In A Bottle   91

The Lilac Tree   94

Going To America   97

Foreword   98

A New Beginning   99

New York   106

Staten Island   115

Bayside, Queens   121

Flushing, Queens 127

Assorted Memories 131

Foreword 132

My Parents Visit Us 133

Good Friends 139

Breakfasts With Hymie 148

Horse Racing 154

Vermont And Other Adventures 157

The Problem With Y's And Z's 160

Denver, Colorado 165

Horst Schafer Photographs 166

The Grandkids' Questions 171

Foreword 172

40 Questions 173

1. Questions About My Life In Germany 174

2. Questions About The War 179

3. Questions About Going To America 182

4. Questions About Life Issues 189

5. Questions About Moving To Colorado 198

Photos of Birgit's Family 204

Photos of Heidi's Family 206

Epilogue 208

Acknowledgements 211

Me on a recent trip to California

I hope my story sheds light on what life was like for me as a young girl and a young woman growing up in Germany during and after World War II. I will also tell you about leaving my home country to go to America and how these events shaped my life.

My stories mostly spring from memory. My recollections are enhanced by what I heard from family members as well as what I learned from researching historical events. This memoir will give you a glimpse into how life was in another time - my time. The stories include happy times as well as times of great hardship. They deal with war and destruction as well as the human spirit to survive and prosper. They also address leaving one's family behind to find a better life far away in America. I hope you will learn about our family and be inspired by the power of human resilience in overcoming adversity. Perhaps you will also get to know me in a deeper, more personal way.

Most of my stories have happy endings, a testament to making the best of what life presents to us. Every day I am grateful for the blessings in my life and for the joy my children, grandchildren and great grandchildren have brought to me.

The impetus for writing this memoir came from my daughters, Birgit and Heidi. From time to time, when I told them stories about the war and my early life, I was told - *with emphasis* - "Mutti, you should consider writing these stories down for us and for future generations. Your experiences during and after the war are so compelling; they are filled not only with your family's struggles but with important historical events and our family's immigration story. Writing it down would be a gift to us all."

A Little About Me

I was born Erika Luise Mannheim on December 28, 1939 in Düsseldorf, Germany. Because of a clerical error that was never corrected, my birth certificate states December 29 as the day of my birth. This is how it happened: My father was so happy to welcome a girl after two boys that he had a drink or two too many to celebrate. The next day, still a bit hungover, he went to City Hall to register my birth. When he got home, my mother looked at the Birth Certificate and said *"But Wilhelm, the date is wrong. It says December 29 but Erika was born on the 28th"*. My father returned to City Hall to correct the mistake. The clerk informed him: *"Herr Mannheim, please understand that it is a very complicated and lengthy process to change the Birth Certificate."* He pleaded with my father to just let it be. Papi was in a good mood and said *"oh well, what difference does a day make anyway?"* And that's how I ended up with two birthdays.

I am the middle child of five children: Erhard, Horst, Erika, Elfriede (Friedel) and Willi. I was a shy, serious girl. I kept my feelings to myself and had private dreams of exploring the world outside of my home environment. I did well in school and got top grades. My mother once said: *"Erika listens very attentively when I tell her something - then she goes and does it her own way. She has a strong mind of her own."* As you will discover, I valued independence and self-reliance from an early age.

Introduction

Long ago

I was that little girl

Just over five years old

Whose house got bombed

And who ate

The heart of a sparrow

For dinner

I'll tell you this and other stories about my life

In the following pages

But let me start from the beginning ...

GROWING UP IN

DÜSSELDORF, GERMANY

My Father ("Papi") Wilhelm Mannheim

My nose senses it first, then my brain registers it - cigar smoke. Every time I smell it, no matter where I am, this vivid memory floods into my mind:

Papi sits at the head of our kitchen table. Dinner is over and the daily newspaper lies in front of him. Mutti is busy tidying up the kitchen, and my siblings have scattered somewhere. I sit across from Papi doing my homework. Out of the corner of my eye I watch as he gets up, opens his personal drawer in the china cabinet, takes out his worn dark brown leather pouch and slowly pulls out a cigar. He closes the drawer and sits back down at the table. He strokes the cigar gingerly and taps it on the table a few times. Next, he snips off one end of the cigar with his silver cigar clipper. He looks at the cigar band, slowly slips it off, and puts it aside.

Now he lights a match, holds the flame to the tip of the cigar and takes a few quick puffs to get it going. He inhales deeply with a quiet pleasure and slowly releases the smoke through his pursed lips. With his thumb and two fingers holding the cigar in front of him, he gazes at the smoke as it slowly curls into the air. He notices that I am watching him. He smiles and deliberately forms perfect rings of smoke with his next exhale. I smile back at him, then quickly lower my eyes and continue with my homework. I sense him settling down and contentedly unfolding the newspaper. When I look up again, I see smoke rising above the pages of the paper. This was a daily ritual - his reward after a long day of work in the factory.

Papi was born Heinrich Wilhelm Mannheim on September 2, 1903 in the German region of Westerwald, a beautiful rural area of green rolling hills dotted with small farms and mineral mines. He died in 1977 at age 74 of lung cancer. He had been a smoker most of his adult life, but gave it up completely ten years before being diagnosed with cancer. Papi was the second of seven siblings, his parents were Wilhelm Sr. (1880-1952) and Emilie Mannheim (1883-1937).

My Mother ("Mutti") Elfriede Krügel Mannheim

Mutti was the glue that held our family of seven together. She was our rock. I have no memory of her being upset or in a foul mood, even while enduring the incredible hardships during and after WWII.

She was born Elfriede Dorothea Krügel on May 21, 1908, in Düsseldorf. She died at age 71 in 1979 after complications from a heart attack. She developed heart problems after the war and later became diabetic. Her parents were Hermann Krügel (1879-1959) and Anna Krügel, born Kessler (1886-1972). Mutti had a younger brother, Alfred. One of my favorite memories of her:

Mutti sits by the kitchen window in our apartment, her feet resting on a small footstool and a large bowl of steaming boiled potatoes in her lap. I stand close by and watch as she peels the potatoes with a small kitchen knife, her hands flying with efficient speed. She looks up at me, takes one of the hot freshly peeled potatoes into her hand, cuts a little slit into the top and slides a piece of butter into the opening.

The butter melts right away and oozes down the sides of the hot, yellow spud. She sprinkles a few grains of salt on top and hands it to me with a warm smile: "Here, Erika, open your mouth wide." The whole potato plops into my waiting mouth. Oh, the taste of the melting butter mixing with the soft potato and salt in my mouth ... heavenly.

My Parents Meet

Mutti was a pretty young woman, blond and blue eyed. I don't know much about her childhood or teenage years as she talked little about that, or maybe I just don't remember hearing about it. I know that she worked as domestic help and for a short period as a switchboard operator (phone operators at that time manually connected phone calls with wires and plugs). She loved that job. I remember her telling me how much she would have liked to work in an office, but that wasn't what young women did back then. Girls were expected to work as domestic help until marriage. Reflecting on this, I believe that her unfulfilled ambition shaped me; it spurred me on to "break the mold" and pursue my dreams.

Papi was a tall, handsome man with blond hair and a serious demeanor. I don't remember him smiling much. As a young man, he saw little future near his hometown and found work as a machinist in Düsseldorf, a large city on the Rhein River, about 85 miles north of where he grew up. In those days, Düsseldorf had a population of about 350,000.

Papi and Mutti met in 1929 at their Lutheran Church choir. Papi was quickly smitten with the beautiful Elfriede and her angelic soprano voice. He impressed her equally with his velvety bass voice, but it took a bit of courting to win her over. Mutti told me once that she had other suitors and at first wasn't that interested in Wilhelm, but he was persistent and eventually stole her heart. They married in 1930.

My parents Elfriede and Wilhelm Mannheim

Years later, Papi joined a men's choir named "Eintracht" (Harmony). I warmly remember his choir singing a love song that eventually became a testament to his love for Mutti. The song is about a young couple in a rowboat as the sun sets into the ocean. The third verse is the one I remember most:

Es Löscht Das Meer Die Sonne Aus

Wie wiegt sich sanft der leichte Kahn,

Liebchen, mit deiner süßen Last.

Als Muschel zieht er seine Bahn,

Die einer Perle Kleinod faßt.

Ach, daß mein Arm die traute Schale wär,

Die dich umschlösse allezeit.

Mit meinem Ruder spielt das Meer,

Liebchen, mein Arm ist dir bereit.

The Sun Sets Into The Ocean

How gently sways our little boat

With you, my love, as its sweet cargo.

Like an oyster shell it slowly carves its way

Cradling you in its hull like a precious pearl.

Oh that my arm the trusted vessel were

To cradle and protect you now and forever.

The sea playfully tosses my oars.

My arm is ready for you, my darling.

Life For My Parents

During their early years as a married couple they experienced the hardships of a country that was dealing with a deep worldwide depression that had started in the US with the Wall Street Crash. Financial markets collapsed, unemployment rocketed, poverty soared and people became desperate.

This fertile ground made it possible for Hitler to come to power in 1933. People eagerly listened to his promises of a better life - especially for the working class who had suffered so much. They listened with great hope and believed his bombastic lies that life would improve under his leadership. Masses of blue-collar workers, including my father, joined Hitler's National Socialist German Workers Party (Nazi). In the early years they were not disappointed. There were plenty of new jobs with good pay and generous benefits for working families, improved housing, wonderful health care and excellent childcare.

I know from conversations with my older brothers that my parents embraced the new leadership, which renewed their hope for our future. They were as horrified as the rest of humanity when the truth about Hitler's evil regime became known. Communication systems were very limited during that time and censored news was slow to get to the public. When people realized the magnitude of what was happening, it was mostly too late to do anything about it. By then neighborhoods were infiltrated by Hitler's spies - neighbors watched neighbors. Anyone caught opposing the government was arrested, jailed or sent to concentration camps.

Our Family Life

Papi and Mutti settled into a small apartment near her parents (Anna and Hermann) in suburban Düsseldorf-Rath. In 1931, they welcomed their first son, Erhard. A second son, Horst, joined their little family in 1935 and I arrived in 1939, just three months after the beginning of World War II. I was the much hoped for girl after the two boys. Did I get spoiled because of that? *Well, if you ask me… of course not!* And don't listen to what my brothers might tell you.

Erhard and Horst are taking good care of me

I only enjoyed being the youngest for a little over three years. In 1943, sister Friedel joined our family. With her blond curls and impish smile, she immediately became the new darling. *Believe me, she was definitely spoiled*, especially since our parents believed that with her arrival, their family was complete.

Fast forward eight years - that's how long Friedel enjoyed being "the baby." A big surprise arrived: Brother Willi entered the world in 1951, twenty years after son number one, Erhard. Willi was born at home. I remember the anxious comings and goings and muffled sounds in our parents' bedroom. Then came a baby's cry, and he was here. Willi was awfully cute and adorable. *Guess who at age twelve was old enough to help take care of this late-comer boy?* I became his surrogate mother, taking care of him while Mutti worked several jobs to help keep our family of seven fed and clothed during the tough years after the war. I did a pretty good job taking care of baby Willi, changing his stinky diapers before school in the morning, feeding him, and playing with him while Mutti was at work.

All was well, except on the day I almost killed him!

That day is burned into my memory and still haunts me sometimes. Willi was just a few weeks old. I carried him from the bedroom into the kitchen when - oh horror - I accidentally hit the soft spot on top of his head hard against the door handle. He stopped breathing and turned blue. Totally panicked, I immediately handed him over to my terrified Mutti (who, thank goodness, was home). She dropped everything and took him from my arms. A great worry showed on her face as she cradled him. I have no memory of what happened next, except that he eventually started breathing again and survived with no brain damage. Today, he is a healthy father and grandfather. Willi and I often reminisce about how I almost killed him.

Baby brother Willi and me

Grown up Willi and me

The Kitchen Table

Life at home mostly took place around our sturdy wooden kitchen table with a durable linoleum top. It had leaves that could extend out if needed and a small drawer on one of the short sides. Mutti kept her wallet and other personal things in that drawer. I loved rummaging through it whenever I was alone, feeling a bit guilty for "snooping." Knowing how tight money was, I imagined secretly sneaking a few bills into her empty wallet. I would have loved to see the surprise and delight on her face when she opened the wallet and saw the extra cash. But of course, since I didn't have any money, that plan never materialized.

Home Cooking

Mutti was a wonderful cook. Oh, the smell of her Christmas goose roasting in the oven. I can still envision her in my mind, bending down and basting that goose with loving care. I adored then and still do today, her sauerkraut with mashed potatoes and wieners (*my mouth waters as I write this*).

Her recipe:

1 large jar or can sauerkraut
2 tablespoons vegetable oil
2 slices bacon, diced
1 large onion, diced
1 tart apple, diced or ½ c applesauce
5-7 juniper berries
white wine

Render the bacon in the oil until crisp, add the onions and sauté till soft, add the sauerkraut mixed with the juniper berries and apple. Add a generous amount of white wine, almost covering the kraut. Without stirring, cook on low heat for about an hour or until the wine is almost absorbed, remove the juniper berries. Now mix it all together and serve with mashed potatoes and your favorite sausage.

We had a ritual for dinner: First, Mutti would serve Papi the choicest piece of meat, then we kids received our share and she served herself last. Sometimes after dinner, Papi would break open a chocolate bar to be shared by all seven of us, each receiving a small piece. While savoring my treat, I sometimes dreamt about how it would be to have an entire chocolate bar to myself. I imagined eating the whole thing in one sitting.

To this day I always keep a stack of Lindt chocolate bars in my pantry, although I have to resist the temptation most times ... *calories, you know*. I love the feeling of abundance, of being able to eat a chocolate bar all at once if I want to. My grandchildren know that there is an endless supply of chocolate for them, *I just can't help it*. One grandchild (Thomas) dubbed me "Shloclate Omi."

Little Rituals

Most nights, Papi sat at the head of that same kitchen table reading the paper and smoking a cigar. When it was time for bed, he waited for all of us to kiss him and Mutti good night. I remember the feeling of his scratchy cheek on my lips. We were each expected to do this every night, even as adults. Other than those goodnight kisses, I don't remember many demonstrations of affection. I have no memory of being told "I love you" or getting hugs and praises for doing well in school. But I also knew without a doubt that they loved me. Words were unnecessary. This wasn't just the way it was in my family, it was how life was. People in those times did not express their feelings as readily as they do today.

I remember Sunday mornings when we kids piled into our parents' bed and Mutti served us breakfast in bed. There were pillow fights and other fun games, lots of squealing and laughter. Our apartment was always bustling with our comings and goings, all seven of us.

Our family had the best parties. Many times our small apartment was filled with friends or relatives; there was always a reason to celebrate. Mutti was renowned for her never-fail remedy for hangovers: marinated herring. There always was a big crock full of the succulent herring ready for anyone who needed it.

As mentioned earlier, Papi sang in a men's choir. We loved going to their rehearsals and concerts. My most memorable concert was in 1957 at the Tonhalle in Düsseldorf, a prominent concert hall. I was 17 and wore a new dress I had made myself: powder blue brocade with a matching evening purse. Later that summer, I wore that same dress and purse at a stenographers' ball where I met my future husband, Horst.

My very favorite song during that concert was the famous waltz "The Blue Danube " by Johann Strauss. I sat mesmerized as the men's voices soared with this beautiful music. Spotting Papi in the large choir made me happy and proud. The music traveled deep inside me and touched my soul. I was so moved that even after all these years I still get goosebumps remembering it.

Reflections

All five of us siblings agree we had a wonderful childhood. Our parents created a loving and caring family environment, even in the face of enormous difficulties and hardships during and after the war. Their love for us was clear, never questioned. They did everything in their power to provide for us and keep us from harm.

1955 - My parents' silver anniversary
Top left: Horst, me, Friedel, Erhard
Bottom left: Mutti, Willi, Papi

2011 - The five of us: Horst, me, Erhard, Friedel, Willi

My Grandparents

Both of my grandfathers served as soldiers in World War I. Later, my father served in WWII.

My paternal grandfather
Wilhelm Mannheim Sr.

My maternal grandfather
Hermann Krügel

On Mutti's side, my Grandfather Hermann (Opa Krügel) came from a poor family of weavers in the northern part of Germany, Schlesien (Silesia) that is now Poland. As a young man, he trekked almost a thousand miles south with only the clothes on his back and a Rucksack (backpack), working day jobs in construction wherever he could find them. This was a common practice in those days. Young men, after completing a three-year apprenticeship in their trade - carpentry, plumbing, construction - traveled around the country and took short-term jobs in their chosen field to improve their skills.

Hermann eventually settled in Düsseldorf, where he met and married Anna. He started a modest construction business with a few tools and a wheelbarrow. Opa was a kind and loving man. He developed Parkinson's disease and died of what is now known as Alzheimer's disease. He often wandered away from home in his demented state. Luckily, when neighbors or church members recognized him, they brought him back home. Back then, we knew little about dementia and how to care for those afflicted by it.

Mutti's mother Anna (Oma Krügel) was a devout Christian and died at 86 of natural causes.

On Papi's side, my grandfather Wilhelm Sr. (Opa Mannheim) worked first as a baker, then at age 34, he became a miner working in an iron ore mine where he labored the rest of his working life. He died of miners' lung disease at age 72. Papi's mother, my grandmother (Oma) Emilie, died at age 54 from a brain aneurysm. Following her death, Wilhelm Sr. married Klara who died at age 46 of a heart attack.

My father's parents lived in a row house near the mines where they kept livestock (chickens, pigs and goats) in the walk-out lower level of their house. My grandparents grew their own fruits and vegetables in a steeply sloping backyard. I have a vivid memory of picking delicious purple plums on one of my visits. I also remember walking my favorite goat to pasture. She became my friend and confidant. While she was busy chomping on grass in the field, I would sit by her side and tell her little secrets.

That's little me riding on top of a cart in the country

A Bit About Those Times

Both sets of grandparents lost their life's savings twice, first after World War I (1914-1918) and again after World War II (1939-1945).

The first currency devaluation was in 1923. After the first World War, the German economy went into a downward spiral. When the government couldn't make its reparation payments, it began printing money in exponentially higher denominations. This created terrible hyperinflation. Day by day, then hour by hour, denominations on the bank notes increased and the underlying value decreased. I inherited some of those old bank notes, ranging in face value from 5,000 Reichsmarks to 20,000, 50,000, 500,000, all printed within a few days of each other. The largest one I still have is for 50,000,000 (yes, 50 million!) On the day it was printed, it would buy a loaf of bread, and the next day it could buy a mere postage stamp. The country went bankrupt and money became worthless. Life savings disappeared, including my grandparents'.

The second currency devaluation was in 1948. Three years after the second world war, many people lost most of their savings overnight when the government instituted a currency reform. From one day to the next, the Deutsche Mark (DM) replaced the Reichsmark (RM) as the new currency. The RM was now worthless, and they gave each living person 60 DM as starting capital. Cash savings were worthless. Bank accounts in the old currency (RM) could be converted to DM at a conversion rate that was a fraction of the original value.

Mutti and her family:
Alfred, Herman, Elfriede, Anna Krügel

Wilhelm Mannheim Sr.
in World War 1

Young Elfriede and friend

I learned many life lessons from my mother; be kind, loving, resourceful, responsible and devoted to family. Yet, these two lessons influenced me the most: meet all of life's challenges with grace and no matter how insignificant the task, give it your best effort.

Elfriede Krügel - Mannheim

Mutti's Creativity With Money

More often than not, money was tight at home. Out of necessity, Mutti was extremely resourceful and creative with family finances. She stretched every Deutsche Mark as much as possible. Mutti's financial resourcefulness was especially apparent at Christmas time. She went to great lengths to assure there would be presents for us under the Christmas tree. Sometimes, when she was short of cash, she pawned whatever she had of value around the house. One year, my sister Friedel and I were the only kids on the block with brand new sparkling roller skates. *Where did she get the money?* Here is the story of how she "financed" those roller skates:

Shortly before Christmas, she took me along to pawn my oldest brother Erhard's good trench coat. The idea was that she would redeem it after Christmas when there was additional money. I was sworn to secrecy. "Erhard will not need his coat until spring," she reasoned. Christmas came, and she beamed when she saw our delight after we spotted the skates under the tree.

Once she had scraped enough money together after the holidays, she again took me along to redeem the coat at the pawnshop. The clerk checked Mutti's claim ticket. "You are a day late. We sold the coat yesterday." Shocked and alarmed, Mutti said, "what do we do now?" partially to me and partially to herself.

Ever resourceful, she said "let's go" and together we rushed to a secondhand clothing warehouse. We searched through rows and rows of trench coats hoping to find one just like Erhard's good coat. After an exhaustive search, we found one that was similar, close in color and a slightly different cut, but it was not close enough to fool Erhard. Tired, we took the impostor coat home. Mutti solved the problem by announcing "Erhard, the cleaners switched your coat by mistake." As I remember, he believed her, and that took care of it - or did it?

A lie is a lie, but I felt the lie was born out of love and therefore acceptable. Now, after all these years, we have a good story to tell and can laugh about it. I believe Erhard still thinks it was irresponsible, but sister Friedel and I think it was resourceful and love our Mutti for it.

Mutti's Work Ethic

During the hard years after the war, Mutti supplemented our father's income by holding several jobs. Early in the morning she peeled potatoes at a factory cafeteria. Some evenings after she made dinner for us, Mutti left again to clean offices at a local business. One time she took me along and showed me how to properly dust furniture. From her I learned to do every job - no matter how small - to my best ability. Her attitude was best expressed by the words of Martin Luther King, Jr.: *"If I cannot do great things, I can do small things in a great way."*

She was known for her high quality work at another job: ironing men's dress shirts for a local laundry. She ironed those shirts until not a single crease could be found. I remember watching her at night while she ironed piles of shirts on our kitchen table, happily singing a tune as the iron swished across the fine cotton, then folding the shirts professionally, including stays in the collars and straight pins holding the folds together. My father's and my brothers' dress shirts were the envy of their colleagues and friends. To this day, I iron shirts the way Mutti taught me (except I do so without stays and pins). First you iron the back, then the sleeves, then the yoke, then the collar and finally the front, being careful not to cause creases.

Laundry days also are engraved into my memory. The five resident families in our building shared the laundry room in the basement. This meant that each family had their turn once every five weeks. As you might imagine - no daily change of underwear for us - maybe once a week. Even at that, the mountain of wash that accumulated by our family of seven was impressive - and more than a bit smelly. My nose clearly remembers the unforgettable "aroma" emanating from the overflowing hamper.

Here's how laundry day went: first, Mutti filled the huge coal-fired kettle with water and laundry soap and let it heat up. When the soapy water was at the boiling point, the whites - bed sheets, towels, underwear - went in first. She stirred the pieces with a long wooden paddle, steam rising until it filled the entire room and she totally disappeared in it. It was hard to breathe in that hot, steamy air. After stirring - agitating - the wash, she lifted the heavy, dripping pieces out of the hot water with the paddle and rinsed them by dunking them from one into a second deep tub filled with cold water. Then she passed everything through a two-roller wringer operated by hand, of course. She repeated the entire process for the dark clothing.

On sunny days she hung the wash out in the backyard to dry. On rainy days she had to carry the wet laundry up three flights of stairs and hang it on clotheslines to dry in the attic. Everything was ironed (no wash'n wear in those days). I already mentioned how meticulous she was with dress shirts, so no cutting corners with her wash, either.

While our mother was busy in the steamy laundry room, we kids played in the backyard and got into trouble running in and out of the laundry that was air-drying on clotheslines. She never yelled at us. Instead, on hot summer days she would bring out a metal tub, fill it with cold water and we had a grand old time splashing and playing in our "swimming pool." She even took time out to make sandwiches for us and delivered them to us by lowering them in a basket from a window.

After the laundry was dry and Mutti had taken it all down, we would use the clotheslines to make tents with old sheets and blankets. They became theater stages where we put on plays of our own making, sometimes charging neighbor kids a "Groschen" (about 5 cents) admittance.

Baby me with Mutti

Howeweg 1
From left: Horst, Erhard, me, Mutti, Friedel

Howeweg 1 - Our Home

(Howe was a German poet, Weg means lane)

Our family lived in an apartment building in a working class neighborhood. The building was part of a large multifamily complex consisting of several blocks of three-story buildings with large shared backyards. Our neighbors were mostly young families with children, which meant lots of friends to play with. The backyards were our playground - extensive lawn areas for running and playing, complete with sandboxes on each block. There were steel posts with hooks for stringing clotheslines and tall metal racks for cleaning rugs. We draped household rugs over the racks and smacked them hard with rattan rug beaters (no vacuum cleaners back then). When those racks were not in use, we kids loved to use them for climbing, swinging, hanging upside down and other gymnastics tricks.

Hardly anyone owned a car in those days, which left the streets available for play. Only service vehicles and street vendors drove down the streets from time to time. I remember the scrap collectors calling: "Lumpen, Eisen, Altpapier" (rags, scrap metal, old paper).

Directly across the street from us was a railroad track just up an embankment. Freight trains rumbled by day and night. Life for us kids took place mostly outdoors, except for school, meals, and bad weather. We had certain "seasons" of outdoor play which we rotated: all kinds of ball games, rope jumping, cops and robbers, hopscotch and shooting marbles. One of my favorites was doing tricks with a diabolo (also known as a Chinese Yoyo). We also loved to fly kites which we crafted ourselves from sticks, colored paper and string.

Our stoves were coal fired and required regular chimney sweeping, so chimney sweeps were a common sight. We considered them our friends and loved watching them as they walked along the roof ridges from chimney to chimney, careful not to slip and fall down the steeply sloping roofs. Setting one foot in front of the other, they moved like tightrope artists. As was the custom, they wore all black, including a black top hat. The long wire brush was propped over their shoulder (remember this from Mary Poppins?). The chimney sweep would lower the brush down the chimney all the way to the first floor. When he pulled it back up a thick cloud of black dust appeared and blackened his face. We cheered them on from below and tried to get their attention. It was generally believed that seeing a chimney sweep brought good luck.

Our Apartment

Our apartment was on the ground floor in the building at the end of our block and just a little over 700 square feet - quite snug for the seven of us. There was a tiny entry with a coat rack, two bedrooms, and a combination kitchen/living room. We shared one bathroom with a toilet and bathtub, no sink. A coal fired stove in the kitchen was used for heating and cooking. There was no heat source in the other rooms. The only sink in the place was in the kitchen, cold water only. Every morning before school or work all of us had to use the kitchen sink to brush our teeth and wash our faces, necks and ears. We took a bath once a week - on Saturdays - which was quite an operation.

Water had to be heated in the coal fired laundry basin in the basement, then hauled up - bucket by bucket - and poured into the bathtub. Several of us took turns in the same bath water.

The Attic Room

When a small attic room became available in our building, the second bedroom downstairs was turned into a living room and the attic room became a bedroom for three of us. Brother Horst got his own bed while sister Friedel and I shared a single bed. Our oldest brother Erhard was often away at state sponsored camps and a boarding school. When he was home, Erhard slept on the couch in the living room. When baby Willi arrived in 1951, he slept in a crib at the foot of our parents' bed.

Friedel and I loved cuddling and tickling each other before going to sleep. We were so used to sleeping together that when I finally had my own bed at age 14, Friedel was very upset. Often, she'd crawl into bed with me. I had to nudge her out gently until she finally got used to sleeping alone.

The attic bedroom had no heat, so it got very cold in winter. We would heat up bricks in the stove downstairs, wrap them in towels and put them under the covers before going to bed. Once in bed we would move the brick to the end of the bed to warm our feet. There was no bathroom. Rather than having to walk down three flights of stairs in the middle of the night, we had a metal bucket (potty) in our room. It was our job to empty and clean it daily, but being busy and lazy kids, it was often a smelly mess *(yuck!)*.

I'll share with you a favorite game we played in our attic room: Spit races (yes, spit races). Two of us would hang out of the dormer window side by side, gather as much saliva as we could in our mouths and start spitting into the groove of a roof shingle (our roofs had grooved red tile shingles). We kept spitting as fast as we could until the saliva stream reached the rain gutter. *You guessed it:* The winner was whose spit arrived first.

The Everything Room

Our kitchen was also our living room. There was a sofa against the wall that also served as seating for the dining table along with four dining chairs. That sturdy dining table was the hub of our family life. Oh, the many stories it could tell. Besides being used for family meals it was: a work counter, ironing table, homework desk, craft table, kneading dough table, baby changing table, sitting around talking table, surprise breakfasts for Mothers' Day table, showing off report cards table, cutting fabrics for making dresses, etc.

Shared Basement

Each family in our apartment building had a stall in the basement which was primarily used to store coal and potatoes in winter plus other items like tools and preserves. Every fall, families would store sacks of potatoes to last all winter. Coal was delivered through a chute, emptying into a large bin.

Built For Bombing Attacks

Our apartment complex was built three years after the start of WWII - around 1942. In anticipation of potential bombing attacks, the basements in each building had one room designated as a bomb shelter. Heavy steel doors sealed the rooms from the rest of the house. The shelters were equipped with benches, tools, gas masks and emergency provisions. In the event of collapse, we could easily break through the thin masonry dividing walls to escape into the adjoining building. When the air raid sirens sounded, we would either go to the basement shelter or head to the closest large community bunker.

In time, we siblings grew up, married and moved away to start our own families. Papi and Mutti lived at Howeweg 1 until they passed away in 1977 and 1979, respectively.

CHILD OF WAR

In the words of beloved poet Mary Oliver, "I would rather die than try to explain to the blue horses what war is. They would either faint in horror, or simply find it impossible to believe."

War is a terrible thing, horrible beyond belief

And always

The people pay the price

War is born of thirst for power by trusted rulers

And always

The people pay the price

War brings destruction, death and misery

And always

The people pay the price

Winners or losers of wars - it doesn't matter

And always

The people pay the price

And always the people

Rise and thrive again

The destruction at the end of WWII

By age ten, I had lived my entire life during wartime and the difficult rebuilding years afterwards. I remember being amazed to hear about places in the world where there was no war, no destruction, where all the houses were standing and people weren't hungry.

In my innocence, war and destruction was just part of life; I simply didn't know it any other way. I was born three months after the start of World War II in 1939. And I was not yet six years old when it ended in 1945. While the following stories revolve around my family and me, they could be the stories of thousands of other families victimized by war.

Even though he was in his forties, my father had been drafted toward the end of the war. Soldiers were dying by the hundreds of thousands, leaving Hitler's army decimated. Rather than surrender, he drafted young boys and older men to fight an already-lost war.

My earliest memories go back to the spring of 1945 - the last weeks of the war and right before Hitler's eventual capitulation. The allied forces (Great Britain, France, the United States and the Soviet Union) mounted massive bombing attacks all across Germany. When it was finally over, my hometown Düsseldorf was mostly rubble, more than 75% of its buildings were destroyed or damaged - including our apartment home on Howeweg.

This is my vivid memory of that fateful day in the spring of 1945 - the day our home was bombed:

The air raid sirens are wailing and wailing, urgently warning us that a major bombing attack is headed our way.

We need to seek shelter right away. Mutti puts two-year-old sister Friedel in the stroller and starts running. Brother Horst (ten) and I (five-and-a-half) firmly grip each side of the stroller and run alongside her. We join the stream of neighbors who are headed in the same direction ... the large community bomb shelter which is less than half a mile away. As always, Mutti carries a small leather valise with important family papers and photos — just in case.

The bomb shelter we were headed toward was built during the early years of the war. It had massive four-foot thick solid concrete walls, and was four stories high with no windows, just small openings for air circulation. It was built to withstand the impact of large bombs without collapsing. Inside the bunker were long hallways and small rooms with cots and bunk beds. A wide sloping ramp allowed masses of people to get in fast. Large, heavy steel doors closed the building.

As we make our way to the bunker, more and more neighbors join the stream of terrified people. There is rushing, shoving, pushing from all sides. I hang on to the side of my sister's stroller, trying to keep up with Mutti's fast pace. We get to a railroad underpass ... the rushing stream of people is jammed together like in a funnel. We are being pressed together and it is hard to breathe. I hold on tight, but all of a sudden -- oh no! -- I lose my grip on the stroller, fall down and am lost among the sea of strangers rushing past me. Where is my Mutti? Where is she?

I am so panicked that I cannot make a sound.

Then I feel someone pulling me up and ... I'm reunited with her ... I am safe again. The whole thing is over in a few seconds, but to me it seems like hours of terror. Safety for me is feeling Mutti's hand in mine and I cling to her hand even tighter. We arrive at the shelter and as we move up the ramp, the mob of frightened people almost pushes me over the railing. Mutti pulls me back with all her strength. We make it to the top just as officials in uniform push us hard inside the already overcrowded building. They shut the heavy doors with a loud bang. We are inside and are waiting anxiously, crammed together with our neighbors.

Soon the low droning, rumbling sounds of approaching airplanes can be heard. The sound gets louder and louder as they keep coming ever closer. We hear the clicking sounds of bombs being released, then the muffled impacts and explosions. It goes on for a long time. The lights in the shelter start to flicker.

We feel the building shake as it gets a direct hit.

Then there is darkness, only flashlights give some light. There is a hushed silence. Everyone is so quiet, holding their breath, holding each other, babies cry, some people pray. Will the shelter hold up? Will our home still be there? Finally, after what seems like eternity, the "all clear" sirens can be heard outside. There is a sudden quiet outside — an eerie silence — it is over.

Slowly, people start to make their way out, anxious to see what it looks like outside. The first fire engine sirens are heard. Mutti and brother Horst follow the others out, leaving baby sister Friedel and me in the shelter for now. "We'll pick you up later," Mutti says. They make their way home - half running, half walking. What will they find? They know that our apartment building is a constant target of enemy fire because it's right next to an elevated railroad track. As they approach our block, they see dust clouds rising from the apartment building. The entire side of the building has collapsed from the impact of a large bomb that left a deep crater a few feet away. Our apartment is a heap of rubble. Everything is destroyed.

We are now homeless.

Bombed out Howeweg 1 after partial reconstruction

Evacuation

We stayed on cots in the bomb shelter for almost two weeks until we found and reunited with my grandparents. Their home also was destroyed and they were relocated into two rooms in the attic of their church's rectory. We lived with them, five people in two rooms with no heat nor running water until we were placed on a train to be evacuated.

I remember the train ride, it was a great adventure for us kids. Sitting comfortably together in our compartment, we were given what seemed like a huge stack of sandwiches, fresh slices of bread loaded with cold cuts and cheese. We were hungry and wolfed them down with delight.

The train went to a rural area in eastern Germany that was largely spared from bombing attacks. People living in those small towns were ordered to take in as many displaced people from the bombed-out cities as they could. Anyone with a spare room or unused attic was ordered to take in evacuees.

Looking back at this today as a mother and grandmother, I can only imagine what it must have been like for my mother, being sent to an uncertain future with three young children and not much more than the clothes on our backs. She had no idea where her husband or her oldest son were.

Was Papi still alive? And what about Erhard? He was faraway in an elite boarding school created by Hitler for exceptional students. Would we see either one again? The school was far away in southern Germany and there hadn't been any communication from him. She didn't know at the time that his school had been abandoned during the chaos of the capitulation and the students had to find their own way home, in Erhard's case, a journey of over 400 miles back to Düsseldorf.

Heart of the Sparrow

For now, we were safe onboard the train. After a long ride, we arrived in the small eastern town of Schönebeck-Felgeleben. The four of us were taken in by a nice family, the Globigs. We lived in a room in their attic.

Food was scarce and we were hungry most of the time. A curfew was in effect which limited the times we could be outside. Mutti and brother Horst dug for potatoes in the fields and anything else they could find to keep us fed. Sometimes they were in violation of the curfew and thereby risking their lives. My little sister Friedel stopped walking, her legs buckling under her from lack of calcium - there was no milk. While many people were close to starving, dead cows with bloated bellies were lying in the fields. The cows were shot by the occupying forces because they couldn't be bothered to milk them.

One day, a sparrow crashed against the window and
fell down dead. Mutti quickly picked him up and
cooked him. That day the four of us shared the roasted
sparrow as our meal. I received his little heart. I still
remember how it tasted ... chewy.

Our life as evacuees revolved around staying alive.

We kids spent most days playing outside. I remember a great day of play acting with my new friends. I was the pretend bride in a wedding. An old tattered white curtain was my veil - there must have been a pretend husband, but no matter how hard I try, I don't have any memory of him - obviously he left little impression. I felt so pretty and important in my wedding outfit. It was a bright and sunny day, warm and pleasant. For us kids, all was well with the world.

One day I noticed my brother Horst racing down the street toward a tired-looking man walking in our direction. "It's Papi, it's Papi!" he yelled with great excitement. We ran as fast as we could and jumped into our father's arms. *Oh, what joy and relief.* We half pushed; half dragged him as fast as we could toward the house. Mutti had heard the commotion and came running, tears streaming down her face. Papi was alive and appeared to be in good health. The little room in the attic now was home to the five of us, and Mutti badly needed help. The only one still missing was oldest brother Erhard.

Papi had been a prisoner of war. He told us about being captured by American soldiers during the last days of the war. They rounded him up with thousands of German soldiers and sent them to the notorious prisoner-of-war camp near Sinzig on the Rhein River. This particular POW camp was known for its brutal treatment of inmates. They rounded men up like cattle with no shelter, no toilets, little food or water. Using their bare hands, they dug holes in the ground for toilets. Hundreds of men died every day from exposure or starvation.

Papi was one of the lucky ones who survived. He befriended some of the American guards by cleaning their toilets and doing other chores. That was his ticket to freedom. After his release, he made his way home only to find our apartment in ruins and no sign of his family. He learned about our evacuation and immediately got on a train to find us. You can imagine our tremendous joy and relief at seeing him.

Shortly after our evacuation, the war ended. In May 1945, the allied forces divided Germany into east and west. They gave the east to Russia. They split the west up between the US, Great Britain and France (Düsseldorf is in the west). Not long after Papi arrived, allied forces occupied the east German town we lived in as refugees. First, American troops marched through the streets and shortly thereafter the Russians came. The American soldiers were kind to us, they were friendly and gave us children chocolate and chewing gum - great treats. Some of the young American airmen loved to scare us, though. They would fly their fighter planes so low over our heads that we would fall down in fear. We could see the pilots laughing as they pulled up at the last moment.

As Russian troops marched in, they jammed the streets with armed soldiers and tanks, instilling fear and dread in the German population. We heard rumors that Russian soldiers were brutal and violent: plundering, beating and raping anyone they wanted.

The Dangerous Border

The Russians created a wide border between east and west Germany - "a no-man's land." No one could cross from east to west. To attempt such a crossing would be to risk one's life. We lived as evacuees in what became east Germany, now occupied by Russian forces. This meant we couldn't go home to Düsseldorf in the west. The Russian border was several miles wide, with soldiers bearing machine guns guarding it day and night. They quickly erected tall watch towers, complete with rotating searchlights to detect any movement and the Russian guards were trained to shoot and kill anyone who tried to cross on sight.

We were now trapped in our own country.

Another nightmare began: Rumors spread that Russian troops in big military trucks stormed into random homes during the dark of night. They kicked down doors, dragged out the men and forced them into the trucks and drove away. Most of those men likely ended up in Siberian labor camps and were never heard from again.

Of course, our parents were terrified that Papi would meet the same fate. They decided not to wait for that to happen and planned our escape back to Düsseldorf, about 300 miles away. Our temporary home with the Globigs was near the new border. For weeks, our parents observed the comings and goings of Russian border guards. They found out when there was going to be a change of the guards. They knew Russians loved their vodka and were counting on them being drunk and distracted during the changing of the guards. They picked a night for our escape that was moonless and totally dark.

Our parents knew that was our best chance for survival.

On the chosen night, our parents gave my two-year-old sister Friedel sleeping pills so she would not cry and Papi carried her in his arms. Mutti, my 10-year-old brother Horst and I carried whatever we could in backpacks, one in front and one on our backs - two packs each. Anything we couldn't carry, we left behind. We had little to begin with, but even a pillow case was precious. Any papers that could be incriminating if we were caught, my parents buried in the backyard. Who knows, maybe that's where they still are today. Here is my vivid memory of our escape:

The tall sugar beet leaves under our feet are crunching, cracking, snapping. Every step is a chore. It is almost totally dark, frighteningly dark. My parents' hushed voices keep reminding us: "sh,sh,sh,sh, don't make a sound." We walk for a long time as quietly as we can with the constant crunch, crunch, crunch under our feet. I feel so tired; all I want to do is sleep. Horst trips over something and falls into a creek bed, getting all wet. He cries, but Mutti quickly hushes him by cradling him in her arms and soothing him with her soft words.

When the search lights come in our direction, our parents pull us down to the ground. "Don't move a muscle," they whisper.

After the lights pass over us and we see them moving away, we continue our march. We walk all night not really knowing where the border ends. Finally, we collapse toward morning in a barn. Are we on the other side? Are we safe? Local farmers discover us that morning in the barn. It amazes them when we tell them where we came from.

"No one else has made it across alive," they tell us.

We are beyond exhausted. We need time for the impact of what happened to sink in. But we now know we are safe, we made it across and we are alive. We are grateful for the food and drink these strangers offer us. Even the mayor of the town comes to talk to us and offers his help to get us home to Düsseldorf.

After a long journey on truck beds and overcrowded trains, we arrived home to our bombed-out house. We found temporary shelter again with my grandparents and were overjoyed to be reunited with our oldest brother Erhard, who had found his way home after his school in South Germany was abandoned. Our family was together again. *It was such a miracle that amid so much destruction, death and danger, our entire family had survived.*

57

The war was over, but the struggle for daily survival had only just begun. The enormous task of rebuilding lay before the survivors - tens of thousands of families were homeless. There was a great food shortage: hunger was our new enemy. So many families had lost loved ones, especially husbands, sons and fathers. Thousands of widows now faced the future alone in the face of unimaginable difficulties.

Rising From The Rubble

After tremendous suffering and hardship the human spirit of survival kicked into full force. The men in our family cleared the debris from inside our destroyed apartment and used building materials they found in the rubble to repair the walls along with windows and doors from other collapsed buildings to create a makeshift home for our family. Soon, the six of us moved into the rooms that were livable, even though rain leaked through the ceiling. We slept underneath open umbrellas on rainy days, but we were home and could slowly start rebuilding our lives.

It took great determination and effort to return to some form of normal life. Many families who lost their homes moved to the countryside hoping to find shelter and food with family or friends.

To little five-year-old me, all these happenings felt normal. I had never known a peaceful intact world. War shaped my life from the time I was born. I had no references or ideas for a different life. War, destruction, and scarcity was my reality. I don't remember feeling sad or afraid; I had my parents and siblings around me. I felt protected and cared for. I do remember hearing the adults talking a lot about "Sorgen" (worries). I wondered what that word meant; "Sorgen." It was not a concept I understood. The adults looked so serious when they talked about Sorgen. I didn't dwell on it. I had the important business of play to attend to.

Most likely my stories and recollections would sound somewhat different if told by my older brothers. Horst was ten and Erhard was fourteen when the war ended. They were old enough to understand what was going on and how dangerous it all was. They remember the fear and horror of their world collapsing all around them. They understood all about "Sorgen."

Innocent Adventures

In 1945, we children enjoyed a long summer without school. The war destroyed or damaged most of the school buildings. Thousands of teachers who fought in the war were dead or missing. While our parents were busy rebuilding our home and searching for food to keep us alive, we had great fun rummaging and playing in the rubble. Oh, the treasures we found... all kinds of broken household items, colorful shards, pieces of pottery, torn bedding and broken furniture. We built forts where collapsed floor slabs had fallen onto each other, creating tunnels and spaces we could crawl into. Playing hide and seek was a favorite activity. We never ran out of secret hiding places.

We felt a bit like adventurers and archeologists digging in the ruins and finding tons of interesting stuff we could use to make up fun games. Being mostly unsupervised, we got into lots of trouble and ended up with scrapes and bruises. Because we were malnourished and mostly barefoot, our injuries festered and were slow to heal. There weren't many doctors around. Mutti had a surefire remedy for those injuries. When we came to her crying in pain, she would put a piece of candy on the wound and say *"as soon as it doesn't hurt anymore, you can eat the candy."*

Many of the bombs that fell on our cities did not explode and precariously lay among the rubble. All of us kids knew about the danger of those unexploded bombs from the constant warnings: *"touch nothing that could be a "blindgänger"* (unexploded bomb). *Stay far away from any objects that are made from heavy metal and are round. Report anything you find that looks suspicious."*

Being kids, we mostly ignored the warnings and rummaged to our hearts' content inside the caves and openings in and around the collapsed buildings. Most of us were lucky, but many children got hurt - or worse - when they couldn't resist playing with interesting objects they found. Often these bombs exploded and maimed or killed children.

Of note: I do not know of kids getting hurt in our neighborhood, but the radio and newspapers frequently reported about tragic events involving children and explosives.

Searching For Food

We were hungry constantly. What showed up in the stores was rationed and hardly enough to feed our family of six. Even when there was enough food in the stores, we could only buy that day's allocation. If the food stamp said four ounces of bread per person, that's all we could buy. There was no guarantee that our grocery store had received enough supplies for all the families. We had to take whatever we could get that day.

I remember all of us sitting around the kitchen table and Papi handing out the rations for the day - each one of us got an equal share: a few slices of bread. a pad of butter, an apple - maybe a piece of cheese. *"It's up to you,"* he said. *"You can eat it all at once or make it last the rest of the day."* I don't remember what I did with my own portions. Did I have the discipline to make it last?

Many families raised rabbits for food. There were cages with little bunnies everywhere. When they were nice and fat, they ended up on dinner plates. All of us kids fed the cute little bunnies with grass and kitchen scraps. They became our pets, and we gave them names. It was a sad day for us when we found a cage empty. Some parents told their children that the rabbit had run away, but dinner that night tasted suspiciously like rabbit stew.

Making Do

When it was my brother Horst's Lutheran church confirmation, we expected family members from the country to help with the celebration. Mutti was planning a sumptuous dinner around a large rabbit roast. For weeks we fattened our rabbit with as much to eat as he wanted. He didn't disappoint… he grew fat and plump. The day before the celebration, Papi came to get him and … the cage was empty, the gate wide open with no sign of the rabbit. Surely, it had to have been stolen. Mutti panicked. What would she serve her guests? She checked with all the neighborhood butchers but there was no meat to be found anywhere. She knew of one more store - a butcher who sold horse meat, a despised option. Horse meat? Unacceptable. Most people wouldn't even consider it and those who did wouldn't admit it.

What was my mother to do? Horse meat was her only option. She went into the butcher shop, looking around carefully. She didn't want to be seen by neighbors or people she knew - in her mind she heard the gossip: *"Did you hear? Frau Mannheim bought horse meat?!"* As mentioned before, Mutti was very resourceful. So she overcame her reservations and bought a large horse meat roast. She cooked it with lots of onions, potatoes, carrots and strong spices to hide the truth. *"Have another helping of rabbit stew?"* she prodded. Were her guests convinced? Reflecting, I have a hunch they figured it out but said nothing out of kindness. And what about the missing fat rabbit? Was it really stolen or was it rescued from certain death by a compassionate family member? We will never know.

The Art of Foraging

There were a few wheat fields nearby where we collected wheat stalks that were left after the harvest. We put them in sacks and thrashed them with sticks to release the kernels, then we ground them in coffee grinders to make flour. Also, we kids collected beechnuts in the nearby woods. We roasted and brewed them to make "coffee." It took quite a stretch of the imagination to detect any flavor resembling coffee. A popular activity was collecting cigarette butts discarded by American troops. Smokers removed the tobacco bits from the butts and rolled them into cigarettes.

To supplement the meager rations and keep our family alive, Mutti and Erhard went to the countryside looking for food. They traveled on overcrowded trains, often standing on the couplings between train cars. People were hanging onto the outside of the trains like bunches of grapes, holding onto whatever they could: door handles, grab bars, etc.

Overcrowded trains with hungry people

In the countryside, after the farmers harvested their fields, they allowed the starving people from the cities to dig up anything that was left in the ground. Digging with their hands, Mutti and Erhard gathered anything they could find, such as carrots, potatoes, beets, and cabbage. On good days, their sacks were heavy, and they happily returned home, again hanging onto overcrowded trains for dear life. It was exhausting and dangerous work, but they were glad it provided full tummies for a while. When the food was gone, they went back to get more.

People took their household possessions to the countryside and traded with the farmers. A crystal candlestick for a pound of butter, a piece of china for sausage, jewelry for meat. We didn't have many treasures like that - most of what we had was destroyed during the bombing.

Winter arrived, and there was no coal for our stove. Erhard would climb up on slow-moving coal trains and toss pieces of coal down to Mutti, who gathered them in bags. The fear of getting caught was nothing compared to freezing in a cold house. One time, Erhard hit Mutti on the head with a sizable piece of coal. She came home bloody but glad to get the stove going, which was not only what kept us warm, it was also where she cooked our meals.

Wooden Spoon

Today, sugar beet syrup is a novelty. I remember there was an abundance of sugar beets one year during those tough times. To make syrup, the beets had to be cooked down for many hours. For days on end, sugar beets simmered on our stove, steam rising from the big, heavy pots. The wallpaper peeled off the walls from all the steam.

Heaven was a slice of bread, a little butter, and a layer of thick, velvety sugar beet syrup. It filled our tummies. The wooden spoon Mutti used to stir and stir and stir those sugar beets still sits in my kitchen drawer, a well-worn precious memento. It reminds me of those times and keeps my appreciation alive for the value of food.

When schools opened again, the allied countries, including America, started a program to feed the school children. I remember standing in line at my school to receive a portion from huge basins of pea, milk or bean soup. The milk soup was especially popular because it contained plump raisins, a special treat. Except one time, just as I brought my spoon to my mouth, I discovered that the raisin was a dead fly - leaving me with a lifelong dislike of raisins.

I remember the miracle of American CARE packages. They started arriving by the thousands and were distributed from warehouses. We heard they contained chocolate and coffee and other wonderful things. I stood in line at one of those places for hours, waiting in vain for a package for my family. With great anticipation, I had visions of coming home with a big package, eagerly opening it and handing out lovely things to my parents and siblings. Only later did I find out that Americans sent those packages to their friends and families in Germany. We didn't know anyone in the US, but then ... hope springs eternal and who is to say there couldn't be the miracle of a long-lost relative who wanted to help us?

Lost In Translation

Cornbread - a common and loved food in America - caused a lot of frustration in post-war Germany. According to the story, an American General asked a German official what the starving people needed most. The answer was "Korn." In German the word Korn is a collective term for grain (wheat, rye, etc.). Understandably, the American General thought we needed the American crop, "Corn". In Germany, the crop Mais (corn) was only raised as animal feed, not for human consumption.

Soon, huge shiploads of corn arrived from the US. Grateful for the help from America but flummoxed, German bakeries ground the corn and set about baking bread, using their normal methods for making wheat and rye bread. The result was a crumbly mess. Eventually, they adapted their recipes, but every German who lived during that time remembers "Maisbrot" (cornbread) with a bit of disgust.

Four years after the war ended, in 1948, things slowly got better. There were jobs and plenty of food. Mountains of rubble had been removed and new buildings went up in record time. Construction was everywhere, especially apartment buildings. Yet, the need for housing was very great for many years to come.

Not Impressed

I was nine years old and had never tasted bananas or oranges because there were no tropical foods during and long after the war. For years, I heard the adults reminiscing about the delights of tropical fruits. *"Wait till you taste an orange or a banana, you won't believe how heavenly they are."* Finally, in 1948, exotic fruits became available again. I had my first taste of a banana. *"Well - is that all there is to it?"* I thought to myself. For me, they did not live up to the hype.

Hindsight

Looking back, I marvel at the ingenuity and industriousness of my parents, especially my Mutti, to keep our family of six fed during a most difficult time. She ruined her health by sacrificing for us and I am convinced that her heart problems and diabetes were a direct consequence of taking care of herself last.

Inspiration On The Kitchen Wall

Mutti's favorite poem hung in our kitchen where it miraculously survived the bombing of our home - its wooden frame and glass still intact. It gave her hope and strength during hard times.

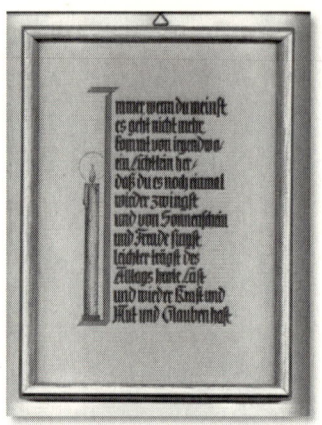

Immer wenn du meinst es geht nicht mehr

kommt von irgendwo ein Lichtlein her

dass du es noch einmal wieder zwingst

und von Sonnenschein und Freude singst

leichter trägst des Alltags harte Last

und wieder Kraft und Mut und Glauben hast

———

Always when you feel you can't go on

a little light appears from somewhere

it lifts you up and helps you face another day

once again you sing of sunshine and joy

and you can face your daily burdens

with renewed strength, courage and faith

Amid all the destruction and misery around us, we neighborhood girls came up with an exciting and satisfying way to amuse ourselves: we built beautiful hidden treasures. First we had to find a good hiding spot underneath some low-growing shrubs or in an out-of-the-way corner; a place out of sight that wasn't easy for naughty boys or rival kids to find.

Once we found the right location we dug a shallow hole in the ground, about the size of a soup bowl. Next we looked for pieces of broken red bricks. We ground them into a fine powder on a rough surface like concrete or street paving. That process took a lot of muscle strength and patience because those bricks were very hard. But we were determined and kept at it until we had what we wanted: a pile of red powder. Next, we lined the holes with this powder, working patiently to end up with a smooth surface that became the background for the next step which was the creative and fun part. We searched around the rubble for all kinds of pretty things: small pieces of colored glass from broken bottles, chunks of porcelain and pottery with pretty designs, mirror shards, buttons, beads — the more colorful the better. We especially loved it when we found bright blue, red, green and yellow pieces.

We arranged them in the prepared hole to create artistic designs and mosaics, pressing the pieces down into the red powder so they would stay in place. Once satisfied with our creation, we looked for a piece of broken window pane large enough to cover the hole. We carefully positioned it on top, secured the margins with dirt, then added a thick layer of soil to protect what was hidden underneath. To disguise our secrets we added small sticks, rocks and leaves so no one would notice anything different. There was no sign of anything special going on under the dirt. We passionately protected our hidden treasures. Only our most trusted friends could come along with us to see them. First, we looked around carefully to make sure no one was watching, then we carefully brushed away the soil until our piece of art appeared in all its glory, glistening in the sunshine - a *thing of great beauty* - in a world of chaos and destruction.

Neighbor girls Hermine, me, Friedel, Renate

Secret Treasures On High Street

Many years later (around 2010) my grandchildren Trevor, Patricia and Shannon were at my house in Denver for a visit. I told them this story, and they loved it. Intrigued, they asked, *"Omi, do you think we could make our own secret treasures in your backyard"*? Delighted, I said *"of course, I would love to show you how."*

We set about looking for suitable items around my house and found colorful marbles, buttons, shiny coins, and small toys. The kids arranged them artistically in plastic boxes and covered them with a clear lid. Then they buried them in the ground after carefully choosing their very own secret spot in the yard. Finally, their treasures were covered with a thick layer of soil, sticks, and leaves.

Being creative and imaginary kids, they carried it a step further and drew up secret treasure maps - complete with burnished edges - like pirate maps. They drew the layout of the yard and an X for the location of their treasure on the maps. They hid the rolled-up maps inside my house so only they knew where to find them (*well...they let me in on their secret*). Every once in a while when they are here for a visit they'd check if their secret treasures are still there... and yes they are, undisturbed underneath a thick layer of garden soil, ready anytime they want to brush away the dirt and check out their very own "thing of beauty."

AFTER THE WAR

Our family after the war

It took many years

Of hardship and struggle

Until life felt normal again

While the world had been dancing in the streets

Celebrating the end of the war

German survivors had been left

With their world torn apart

I was in my teens

When things returned to normal

When we could

Go about our lives

In ordinary ways

We survived and thrived

Money, or the lack of it, made a large impression on me during my childhood. The lack of "enough" money was ever present in my family. As mentioned before, Mutti handled our household finances and was often short, barely scraping together enough to pay the bills. When buying on credit became available, she made use of it and sometimes was late on her payments. Observing this caused money matters to become important to me at a young age. I became a saver early on and believed in the importance of living within one's means.

Charms Of The Store

When I was about ten years old it became my job to do most of the grocery shopping, which I didn't mind at all. In fact, I really loved going to our neighborhood grocery store - it was such a magical place and full of mystery to me. I remember the sound of the doorbell when entering, the squeaky wooden floors, the heavy dark wood paneling, and the tall wall-to-wall wooden shelves and drawers. Sitting on the floor were large barrels filled with all kinds of goods - fruits, vegetables and household items. Wooden drawers of all sizes were labeled with their contents, really big ones at the bottom and smaller ones higher up. The tall wooden counter instilled a sense of awe and mystery in me, especially before I was tall enough to see over it.

How I longed to be on the other side of that counter. I wanted to be the store clerk; I envied them for being able to open the drawers and scoop out sugar, flour, rice and beans. I watched as they'd pour the contents into cone shaped brown paper bags which were placed on top of big scales to weigh the proper amount for the customer. Finally, they closed the bags by folding the pointed tops down with precision, then folding the sides down securely and laying them on top of the high counter in front of the customer asking, *"What else may I help you with?"*

Best of all was the big cash register. This was a machine of wonder and fascination. It sat tall and shiny at the end of the counter and I dreamt about how wonderful it would be to punch those shiny keys and hear the ring of the bell when the cash drawer opened to reveal its compartments filled with bills and coins. I imagined how important I would feel to be handed cash by the customer and count out the correct change into their waiting hands.

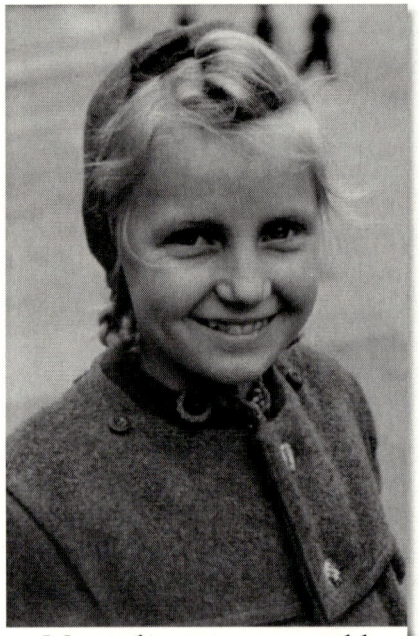

Me at about ten years old

Daydreaming aside, my job was to buy the items on the list Mutti handed me. When it came time to pay, I was instructed to say *"anschreiben bitte"* (on credit please). I suspect that the reason Mutti sent me to do the shopping was probably because she was ashamed to say the words *"on credit"* herself, admitting that she didn't have the money. It was easier for her to send me. Who could deny such a cute and serious little girl? And as far as I know, she always paid up in the end.

The storekeeper knew me, of course, and couldn't help but notice how fascinated I was with the things that went on in his business. One day he said to me: "Erika, when you are finished with school, you can work here." *Did I hear right? This important man wants me to work for him? - In this beautiful store?* I couldn't think about much else for a long time. On that day, I thought my life was all set. I felt very special and accomplished.

Lessons From Shooting Marbles

Although I had my ambitions of becoming a grocery store clerk, I was also very good at shooting marbles. Ours was not a world of pretty glass marbles. Our marbles were made from fired clay, round and smooth, in all kinds of earth colors.

We carried our marbles in cloth sacks with drawstrings and guarded them carefully. I was very good at shooting marbles and kept beating my friends.

The goal of each game was to win the opponent's marbles. I did a lot of winning and my sack became fuller and fuller and theirs, well, you know - soon they were out of marbles. That's when the entrepreneur in me kicked in. *"I'll sell you some marbles, 1 Pfennig (1 cent) a piece."* That way we were back in business and could keep on shooting marbles. And, you guessed it - I kept on winning.

The whole thing repeated until there was a lot of jingling in the bottom of my sack and my friends were out of marbles *and* money. I loved the sound of the marbles mixing with the coins and didn't feel a bit sorry for the losers. Afterall, it was strictly business, right? It wasn't my fault they played so badly. And, didn't I do them a favor by giving them a chance to get their marbles back?

My family believed I inherited my business sense from my grandmother - Oma Krügel. She was known to charge her guests for taking a bath at her house. Afterall, electricity to heat water costs money, right?

Christmas At Home

I'm overcome by a deep sense of joyful nostalgia whenever my thoughts wander back to the Christmases of my childhood. To this day, the memories of the exquisite anticipation and joy are so strong that I cannot sing "Silent Night" without tears welling up.

The four of us: Erhard, Horst, me, Friedel

As children, we experience the world in magical and wondrous ways. Our pure innocence and imagination help us ignite beautiful worlds around us, filled with surprises and wishes coming true. That is how I remember Christmas at home.

We had little during those years after the war, but our parents, especially Mutti, used their loving ways and resourcefulness to create true magic for us. On the days before Christmas, our anticipation grew with each muffled sound of secret preparations behind closed doors - it was such sweet torture.

Many things were still scarce, including the traditional candles for the Christmas tree. Real candles, the ones that fit into special metal candle holders with clips that are fastened to the tree branches, were a valued tradition. Papi and Mutti could not accept Christmas without real candles for our tree, so they made them from scratch. In the months before Christmas, they collected wax scraps wherever they could find them and Papi made candle molds by hand from scrap metal. He poured the melted wax into the molds, put a piece of string in the center as a wick and let it set. The resulting candles were crooked and kind of grayish brown, but they served their purpose.

I loved making Christmas ornaments from gold foil and straw and other materials I found around the house. My masterpiece was a beautiful "Rauschgoldengel" (tree top angel). I fashioned her head out of softened wax and glued shredded wool to her head for hair. How proud I would be to see her gracing our Christmas tree that year. While working on my angel, delicious aromas filled the air from the kitchen where Mutti and brother Horst, the pastry chef, baked mountains of cookies. I still use some of those recipes today; the recipe for the traditional spice cookie "Spekulatius" is at the end of this story.

On the last days before Christmas Eve, our living room was off limits. Pressing our ears to the closed door, we could sometimes hear quiet activity and hushed voices inside. The anticipation intensified with each day that passed.

Silent Night

I especially remember one of those Christmases:

I must have been nine or ten years old. As always, we attended Christmas Eve service at our church, the

"Dankeskirche," a thirty-minute walk from home. Our beloved pastor Halfmann led the service. His jubilant and powerful voice rang clear above us all in singing the familiar hymns. Oh, how hard it was to sit still. We children fidgeted in our seats and couldn't wait for it to be over. Images of presents dancing around in our heads. Will I get the roller skates I have wished for so long? Maybe a new doll? Dare I hope for a bike?

Finally, after the rousing "Oh Du Fröhliche" (Oh You Joyful), we were on our way out of the church. Why was everyone moving so slowly? "Stop pushing, wait your turn." Outside, the winter night was crisp and clear, it was dark and so very quiet. The stars seemed to shine brighter than usual. Walking along, we could see the outlines of lit Christmas trees behind curtained windows and silhouettes moving about. "Can't we go a little faster?"

When we arrived home, our grandparents warmly greeted us. Opa Hermann and Oma Anna, who had arrived while we were in church, welcomed us dressed in their finest. It was warm in the house and smelled heavenly. We waited impatiently in the kitchen until finally the little bell rang telling us that "Christkindchen" (Christ Child) had finished her work (in that part of Germany, the Christ Child, a beautiful angel, brought the presents, not Santa Claus).

Slowly, agonizingly slow, the living room door opened and there it was - the Christmas tree in all its glory with its candles lit, its boughs filled with homemade ornaments, tinsel, strung-up cookies and candy and my handmade angel sitting on the top branch.

There were presents under the tree for everyone, no fancy wrappings - a little pile of things covered up with a plain cloth. On the table were special Christmas paper mache plates filled with cookies, candies, apples and oranges, each with a name tag. We kids did a quick survey of the plates out of the corner of our eyes. We had to make sure there wasn't an extra cookie or candy on someone's plate. Ok - three foil wrapped chocolate balls, one chocolate angel, four cookies, two apples, one orange - yes, ok, everyone had the same.

We stood as a group, admiring it all and singing carols: "O Tannenbaum." (Oh Christmas tree) "Stille Nacht, Heilige Nacht" (Silent night) - my parents with their lovely voices, Mutti's clear soprano and Papi's strong bass with us kids doing the best we could. Oma Anna's enthusiastic but a bit scratchy voice could be heard over us all. We kids were impatient for the singing to stop so we could finally get to our presents. When it was my turn, I found my first doll under the tree, a baby doll with no hair. I felt a pang of disappointment because I had dreamt of a girl doll with wavy hair that I could comb and braid. But like any good mother, I learned to love the baby doll and named her "Pusselchen."

After the "Bescherung" (receiving of gifts) we crowded around the kitchen table to share a yummy meal of potato salad and wieners, followed by "Mohnpielen," a traditional German Christmas dish handed down from our great grandparents who grew up in the German region "Schlesien" (Silesia) which today is Poland. The dish consists of white bread chunks soaked in milk, raisins, nuts and lots of poppy seeds.

Christmas morning was a time to show off our new toys to our friends on the block. All the children were out in the street with their new doll carriages, scooters, balls, roller skates, new shoes and dresses. Soon a bit of competition was going on: "*mine is better, faster, bigger than yours.*"

The memory of Christmas at our home will always stay with me. I have tried over the years to create a similar experience for my children and grandchildren. I feel great joy and gratitude when we are all together around the Christmas tree, complete with real candles. My heart is glad when I see the smiling faces and excitement of the little ones and the love we share as a family.

Granddaughter Carli lighting the tree candles

Spekulatius Cookie Recipe

3 cups all-purpose white flour
1 cup cornstarch
1 cup ground almonds
2 teaspoons baking powder
1 cup sugar
2 large eggs
2 tablespoons milk
1 cup soft unsalted butter
1 pinch salt
1 teaspoon vanilla extract
½ teaspoon almond extract
1 tablespoon unsweetened cocoa
½ teaspoon anise powder
½ teaspoon ground cloves
½ teaspoon cardamom
1-½ teaspoon cinnamon

Cream the butter and sugar, add eggs and milk, beat till incorporated. Add flour and all dry ingredients, mix till a firm ball forms. If too dry add more butter. Wrap dough in plastic wrap and refrigerate at least one hour, roll out very thinly and cut out shapes with cookie cutters.

Bake at 350 degrees F for ten minutes until golden brown. Store in airtight containers.

How We Met

I almost missed meeting Horst, my future husband, because I didn't want to go to the dance. What would have happened if my persistent friend Annemarie hadn't been able to convince me to go with her to the Stenographers' Ball?

It was 1957, I was 17 and working as an office clerk. Annemarie and I had just completed a course in typing and stenography (shorthand). I hoped that proficiency in those skills would open career opportunities for me as a secretary. To celebrate graduation, the business school invited us to a ball at the Rheinterrasse, a fancy party venue on the banks of the Rhein River.

Unconvinced, I said to Annemarie *"I don't think I'll go ... there'll be mostly girls as boys don't take shorthand,"* I continued; "*It'll be boring."* The lack of young men wasn't a problem for Annemarie, she had a boyfriend to escort her. "Oh come on, the three of us can go together, we'll have a good time." She kept insisting, so I finally relented.

We wore our best dresses. Mine was the baby blue brocade dress I wore to my father's choir concert earlier that year. The three of us sat near the dance floor. Annemarie and her boyfriend chatted happily and had a great time dancing. I felt self conscious and out of place because my two companions were busy with each other and mostly ignored me.

But then, when I least expected it, a young man stood in front of me and asked *"May I have this dance?"* His name was Horst, he was handsome with auburn hair and large blue eyes. He had a great smile and was a wonderful dancer. After that first dance he asked me over and over again. We twirled around the dance floor all night, not missing one dance. He held me firmly in his arms and confidently led me in all the different dances of the time: Foxtrot, Vienna Waltz, Cha Cha Cha and Tango.

I felt secure in his arms but wondered if it was normal that he held me so tight? I glanced across the room and noticed that other couples allowed a bit of space between them. Was it all right that our bodies were so close together? I calmed my reservations by deciding that Horst wanted us to move in real unison, so I relaxed and enjoyed it. Annemarie and her beau were quickly forgotten, we hardly saw them anymore.

All the dancing made us hot and sweaty, so Horst suggested we take a walk outside in the gardens. Just like in a romantic movie scene, we walked through the open French doors onto the grand terrace and strolled through the pretty gardens. The summer air was balmy and fragrant with flowery scents. He guided me to a secluded bench and we sat down. I could feel my heart beating and I didn't know how to act. I didn't have to worry, though, Horst knew exactly what to do when he wrapped his arms around me and lightly kissed me. He must have liked it because he kissed me again and again.

When we returned to the dance hall, it was almost empty; even Annemarie and her boyfriend didn't wait for us. And the rest, as they say, is history.

Our first date after that night was at Triton's fountain in downtown Düsseldorf near the Königsallee, a well-known shopping and dining street with fancy shops and outdoor cafés, similar to Rodeo Drive in Beverly Hills. Neither he nor I remember what we did that day after meeting at the fountain. But we set up another date and decided I should meet him close to where he lived, in the southern suburb of Düsseldorf called Benrath. I lived all the way across the city in the northern suburb, Mörsenbroich (Rath). I wore a pretty new dress that I made myself and I took the Strassenbahn (streetcar) to meet him, about an hour's ride away.

As I approached my stop, I saw Horst through the window. He stood there with his bicycle and gave me one of his big smiles as I jumped off the Strassenbahn to meet him. I hopped on to his bike's crossbar and off he pedalled to the banks of the Rhein river. After crossing on a small ferry, we rode to a nearby lake to enjoy the picnic he brought along. We spread a blanket under a tree and did what young sweethearts have done and still do all over the world; we made out ("knutschen" in German) and talked about many things.

Horst was my first real boyfriend - I found him very attractive and interesting. I admired his intelligence: he could talk for hours about atoms and protons and other scientific things I never heard of. I was fascinated by all of his knowledge. I only had an eighth grade education and eagerly soaked it all up. He had the equivalent of a high school education and loved to share what he had learned.

My new sweetheart also helped me to improve my dancing. He knew all the fancy steps and taught them to me. We practiced at his parents' apartment, without music, but with skill and determination. I was impressed with his photographic talent: he had such an eye for composition and beautifully captured everyday scenes such as slender stems of grass peeking up from the snowy ground, an old man pulling a handcart, and the rising shape of a modern office building.

His goal was to make a career in photography. He didn't think he needed formal training and planned to teach himself what he needed to know. I was very taken by his maturity. Horst was 24 - seven years older than me. He told me about his solo bicycle travels to France and England and about his plans for a trip around the world. He spoke decent English and French. I met his friends and we went to lots of parties.

On New Year's Eve that year we celebrated with friends, including the German custom of "Bleigiessen" - lead pouring; a tradition-based activity designed to predict the future. A special spoon is used to melt a small lump of lead over a flame. When the lead liquifies, it is quickly poured into a bowl of cold water. The lead hardens instantly and takes on interesting shapes that are interpreted as predictions for what is ahead in the next year. My lump of lead clearly showed a flaming heart. I still have it and keep it as a treasured memento.

We married the following Spring, on May 17, 1958. Birgit was born on October 3rd. Having a baby at age 18 was sooner than planned and it changed both of our lives' trajectories. But it also fulfilled a dream I had as a young girl: above all else I wanted to become a mother.

We immediately fell in love with our most adorable baby girl and named her Birgit Elke. She was the first grandchild for Horst's parents and instantly cherished. I could tell that, like me, she definitely had a mind of her own from the moment we brought her home.

Strange how often our entire lives change because of one decision. Is it pure chance or is it fate? Would I have stayed in Germany if I had not met Horst on that summer night in 1957?

Our wedding in 1958

Music In My Life

Classical music is my constant companion. I listen to it on the radio when I am at home and in the car. I enjoy my extensive collection of classical CDs. I can sit in one spot for hours just listening to a favorite piece, often an opera. I miss my music when I'm away and can't wait to turn on the classical music station the moment I get home. Listening to music calms my soul and takes me to places of peace and contentment as few other things can. I don't feel lonely or anxious while listening to a favorite symphony, concerto, or opera.

My earliest recollection of being introduced to music was hearing my mother sing. Mutti had a lovely soprano voice and often sang while doing her normal chores around the house. One of her favorites was this folk song by Franz Schubert:

Der Lindenbaum
Am Brunnen vor dem Tore,
Da steht ein Lindenbaum.
Ich träumt in seinem Schatten
So manchen süssen Traum
Ich schnitt in seine Rinde
So manches liebe Wort
Es zog in Freud und Leide
Zu ihm mich immer fort

———

The Linden Tree
At the well outside the gate,
There stands a linden tree.
In its shade I dreamt
Many a sweet dream
In its bark I carved
Many a word of love
In joy and in sorrow
I was drawn to it

Opera

Mutti was an opera lover. Each year she bought season tickets to the Düsseldorf Opera. Papi didn't have any interest in opera, but my cousin Wolfgang was a fan so he and Mutti became opera buddies.

When I was 17, Wolfgang couldn't make it to a performance, so Mutti invited me to join her for Puccini's *La Boheme.* I remember feeling so special to be among so many opera lovers - a brand new world of elegance and sophistication. The beautiful music and the tragic love story of Mimi and Rodolfo touched me and planted a seed that grew steadily into a lifelong passion for this form of music.

My love for Mozart also began around that time. When Horst and I were dating, his first Christmas gift to me was Mozart's "Eine Kleine Nachtmusik" (A Little Night Music). To this day it is still one of my favorite pieces of music.

In our married life, I was on my own with my love for opera, as Horst was more into jazz. He did like some classical music but couldn't tolerate opera. When he was home, we had a bit of a friendly battle going on — classical music or jazz? Often I let him win, unless it was time for Saturday's opera broadcasts.

Horst would lecture me: *"I don't understand what you get out of opera, the singing is artificial and contrived. I can't stand the screeching female voices. They hurt my ears, they are totally unnatural. Can't you see that jazz is natural, organic and unstructured? Jazz musicians get together, feed off each other through improvisation and create great organic music."*

I of course responded, *"But Horst, don't you see there is nothing artificial about the way classical singers develop their voices? They train their vocal cords like a precious instrument. There is nothing artificial about that."*

And he'd come back with, *"Well, opera stories are totally ridiculous and stupid, they are the worst soap operas. They insult my intelligence. Jazz is honest and down to earth, it's spontaneous and pure. Nobody gets murdered, lied to, abandoned or worse."*

But still I defended opera, *"You just don't get it. Operas express human emotions in a way no other art form can. The arias of love, loss and joy go straight to your soul. One deeply feels the characters' pain, their hopes and their happiness."*

We agreed to disagree and tried our best to compromise. Horst usually listened to what he wanted when he was home; I figured I had many more opportunities to indulge when he was at work. After living in New York for two years, we were able to buy a Telefunken HIFI stereo system. I discovered the classical music station WQXR and listened to it constantly. I especially looked forward to the Saturday afternoon live opera broadcasts by the Metropolitan Opera. Those broadcasts are one of the longest playing radio programs which I still listen to today, so many years later.

Opera programs from my
Mutti

Sister Friedel and me in Paris

14 Angels

Some years ago, when my sister Friedel visited me in Denver, we had an intimate talk about our lives and shared feelings about our "final curtain call." How surprised and delighted we were when we discovered that, independent of each other, we had selected the same piece of music to be played at our memorial service: The beautiful evening prayer from the opera Hänsel and Gretel by Engelbert Humperdinck. It's a short, sweet song about protection and faith that never ceases to make me feel glad.

14 Engel

Abends wenn ich schlafen geh

Vierzehn Engel um mich stehn

Zwei zu meinen Häupten

Zwei zu meinen Füßen

Zwei zu meiner Rechten

Zwei zu meiner Linken

Zweie die mich decken

Zweie die mich wecken

Zweie die mich weisen

Zum himmlischen Paradeisen

---

14 Angels

When at night I go to sleep

Fourteen angels watch do keep

Two my head are guarding

Two my feet are guiding

Two are on my right hand

Two are on my left hand

Two who warmly cover

Two who o'er me hover

Two to whom it's given

To guide my steps to heaven

Something extraordinary happened to me in 1955. A postcard arrived from Holland addressed to me: "*We found your bottle and would like to meet you.*"

My hometown Düsseldorf lies along the banks of the mighty Rhein River. After leaving the city, the Rhein flows northwest for about 100 miles where it crosses the border into Holland and eventually flows into the North Sea at Amsterdam.

While picnicking with my family on the river bank, I remembered a love story that started from a message in a bottle. I was fifteen years old at the time, and thus a romantic idea was born: I wrote a note with my name and address on a piece of paper, stuck it in an empty bottle and tightly secured the stopper. I didn't want it to get tangled up along the shore, so I took a running start and flung the bottle with all my strength as far into the fast-flowing river as I could.

I saw it bobbing along the current for a minute until it was out of sight. How exciting and fun. My imagination produced all kinds of scenarios. How far would the bottle travel? Would anyone find it? Would they contact me?

Days, then weeks, then months went by and nothing came from it. I thought my bottle must have broken or gotten stuck in the river's undergrowth. What were the chances, really, of someone finding it? I was disappointed and forgot about it.

Until one day the postcard arrived in the mail, postmarked in Holland: "Hi, we found your bottle and would like to meet with you. Please write to us where and when. We are two friends, 17 years old and live in Arnhem, Holland." Are they girls or boys? I knew enough Dutch to figure out that their names sounded male. Two teenage boys - let the romance begin. I was beside myself with glee and knew I had to see them. This was too exciting.

I wrote back with a date and time where I - together with a girlfriend - would meet them on the banks of the river.

On the day of our arranged rendezvous, I asked Mutti, "Edith and I are biking to the Rhein, can you pack a picnic lunch for us please?" Well, Mutti was all the wiser. *"All the way to the Rhein, that's a long ride. Any special reason?"* "No," I responded, *"We just want to have a fun afternoon."* Mutti looked at me quizzically *"By any chance, does this have something to do with the postcard from Holland?"* Oh shucks, my plan was exposed. No use now trying to hide the truth. *"Let me get this straight,"* Mutti said. *"You two are meeting two strangers, young men whom you know nothing about, from another country to boot. Something smells really fishy about this."*

"Oh please, Mutti, we are not little kids. We are 15 and responsible. Have we ever caused you to distrust us?"

This negotiation went on for some time. Then Mutti, who remembered being young once, agreed to let us go but with one condition: my younger sister would come along. *Oh what a blow* - An 11 year old chaperone? Friedel was practically a baby, childish and needy. She'd be a turnoff for these sophisticated young gentlemen from Holland. My romantic dreams took a serious hit. But I knew it was useless to continue arguing. Friedel was coming along.

As we pedalled along that beautiful late summer day, I was full of anticipation. What would the boys be like? Good looking? Nice? Would they speak German? I only knew a few Dutch words. Then a nagging thought: If only we could get rid of our chaperone. I loved my little sister, but I didn't want her with me on that day.

The boys were waiting for us as planned. They were *handsome* and *nice* and told us *in German* how they had been exploring along the shore of the river outside their town when they spotted the bottle. It was caught in some debris at the water's edge. Curious, they waded in and pulled it out. They could see the paper inside and popped the cork. There was my note, still dry and clearly readable.

Too bad Friedel's presence spoiled everything. How can you have a grown-up conversation, never mind a little flirting, with a baby sister grabbing for attention? We had our picnic with the boys and talked some more, then we biked home.

I never heard from the Dutch boys again. Mutti spoiled what could have been a movie-worthy love story. Two handsome boys from Holland and two beautiful German *Fräuleins*, brought together by a message in a bottle that traveled over one hundred miles in our beloved river Rhein.

A missed chance of a lifetime?

The Lilac Tree

Every spring, the lilac tree outside our home on Howeweg grew taller, its branches reaching up to our bathroom window, loaded with lovely fragrant purple flowers in spring. To this day, whenever I see a lilac tree, it brings back memories of home. One of those memories is sad, however. It reminds me of that day in 1977, the last day I saw my father alive:

Papi is standing in the open bathroom window, his right hand raised in farewell. The lilac tree next to the window completes the image in my mind. He looks pale. I wave back from the car as my brother Willi slowly drives away to the airport, where I will catch my flight back to Denver. As I lose sight of Papi in the window, tears start rolling down my face and Willi reaches across to comfort me. The knowledge that this is the last time I will see my father wears heavily on me. He passed away not long after that visit.

Before that fateful day, brother Erhard called me in Denver: *"Papi is very ill, we believe it is a matter of time until he loses his fight with lung cancer... can you come home to see him?"* He also told me not to discuss the real reason for my visit. *"Papi still believes he just has a severe case of bronchitis. He doesn't know it is cancer. We'll just tell him you were on a business trip to Germany and could arrange a side trip to visit family before flying back to Denver."* I immediately booked my flight.

When I arrived, Papi was frail, but as always, he was happy to see me and appeared in good spirits. It was common back then that patients weren't told the truth about their terminal illness, presumably to spare them from living in anticipation of the end.

Everyone in my family knew what was going on and I had no choice but to play along. Knowing it would be the last time I saw him alive, it was terribly difficult not to be able to hug him and tell him that I loved him (it was not common practice to openly show our affection; doing so would have made him suspicious). I was very glad I got to see him, but sad I couldn't have a final father/daughter talk with him. I believe deep down he knew what was going on but didn't want to upset me. So I left him with a heavy heart. Forever stored in my memory is the image of Papi, standing in the open window by the lilac tree, waving goodbye.

In remembrance of him I planted a lilac bush in my backyard in Denver. Whenever it catches my eye, I like to let my thoughts wander to the lilac tree of my youth, most especially in spring when the purple blossoms open. It reminds me of a happy home, a childhood filled with the comings and goings of a large family.

Whenever I visit home, I go back to our old neighborhood as often as I can, just wandering around the buildings, remembering and reminiscing. In my mind, I see Mutti leaning out the window, framed by the lilac tree, calling us to dinner: "Erika, Friedel, Willi, Horst, *Essen kommen*" (time to eat). The buildings have been refurbished in recent years and don't look as drab as in my youth. There are now fresh coats of paint, new and larger windows, new doors and lush landscaping.

When we were little, the lilac tree was just a seedling, but it grew taller every year - even making it through the bombings of the war. Its branches were torn off, but just like us, it too was a survivor. New branches grew and flourished again from its inner strengths. I often think of that lilac tree and what it symbolizes. Every year in spring I watch out for those first buds to appear on my own Lilac tree.

Mutti and Papi looking out of their kitchen window
The Lilac tree branch to the left.

GOING TO AMERICA

Foreword

Migration, emigration, immigration
As old as human existence
Leaving one's home country
Starting anew in a foreign land
Spurred on by dreams and hopes
The promise of a better life

Horst and I became such wanderers
Restless at home
Dreaming of more ...
What was this allure
To begin anew – to start over?
When and how did it
Take on the form of actually doing it?

Why did we reject the comfort of
Staying close to family
In familiar surroundings
And predictable futures?

Why did we yearn for change
Risking failure and disappointment?
How would we adapt to a new language?
How would we fit in with people of
Different values, unfamiliar customs?

Being young, enthusiastic, confident and filled with hope
We disregarded our reservations
And just went for it

Hello America

A New Beginning

In 1958 the war had been over for many years, but its effects were still being felt. Lack of housing was still an enormous problem. Reconstruction could not keep pace with the demand. What that meant for Horst and me as newlyweds and parents of baby Birgit was an almost hopeless situation to find an apartment. Horst's parents, Alma and Max Schäfer, took us in and we lived with them in cramped conditions: four adults and a baby in a small apartment (kitchen, living room and bathroom). Alma and Max slept behind a curtain in the kitchen, while Horst and I shared a couch in the living room. Baby Birgit had her own crib and wasn't aware of any hardship because she had four loving adults seeing to her every need.

Horst's efforts to make a living as a photographer weren't getting much traction. Photography wasn't considered "proper work." Our families watched this with concern and started to "encourage" him to do something else, anything that would give him a steady income to support his family. But Horst was passionate about photography - it was his calling. Soon he set his sights on a much bigger dream, a daring plan to move his family far away from the challenges at home.

One day he said with excitement: *"Erika, let's try our luck in the New World - America. I hear that there are unlimited opportunities in New York for people like me. There is a great market and appreciation for fine photography. I know that's where I'll have a real chance of making it. I must be free to explore opportunities without the constant scrutiny of family. I understand that they only want what's best for us, but taking any kind of job would be the end of my dreams. I am confident in my abilities as a photographer and New York is where I know I can make it."*

My adventurous side was excited and I could already imagine the tall skyscrapers of New York in my mind, the Statue of Liberty and ocean liners docked in the harbor. But my practical side pulled me back into reality.

I asked him, *"But Horst, we have baby Birgit, very little money and I only know a few words of English. How could we possibly make it?"*

He replied, *"Erika, we just have to try it. I know we'll make it somehow."*

I continued, *"Where will we get the money for the passage? How would we get a visa with so many other young people wanting to emigrate? I think the United States has a strict immigration quota and there are all kinds of tough requirements like proof of employment, financial independence or an American sponsor. I don't see that we have any of those. I certainly could not work because I have to take care of Birgit. It would take a long time for me to learn enough English to get by."*

He assured me, *"We will just take it step by step. You'll see we can make it work. We'll figure it out along the way."*

I needed convincing. *"I don't know - how sad it will be to leave our families. How long would it be before we could see them again? Our parents will be heartbroken if we take their grandchild so far away."*

Horst challenged me. *"Erika, where is your sense of adventure? One thing I love about you is your open mind to new things, you are ready to try most anything. Just imagine all the new things you'll see and do. New York is a fascinating place where people from other countries are welcome. There will be more opportunities for us than we will ever have here at home."*

As his reasonings grew on me, my reservations and fears were gradually replaced with excitement. Then an old and vivid memory flooded back to me.

It is 1952, I am 12 years old and standing outside the chain-link fence that surrounds the Düsseldorf International Airport. I love watching the comings and goings of people and planes. There is an excitement about it, a wonder about flying in an airplane, going to faraway places. I can't help but dream about being on one of those planes.

My eye catches some activity on the tarmac, near to where I am standing: A four engine propeller airplane, its engines running, is ready to board. The gangway is lowered to the ground, waiting to receive the passengers. A loudspeaker announces: "Flight so-and-so to New York is ready for boarding." One by one the passengers emerge from the terminal building. They walk single file toward the plane and climb up the stairway.

And that's when I spot her - a girl about my age - walking confidently toward the gangway. Now she climbs up the stairs and disappears into the plane. I am fascinated. My heart is pounding and my thoughts are racing: What if I could be that girl? What if that was me going to New York on an airplane? How I envy her. I can't take my eyes off this scene and watch the plane as it slowly ascends into the sky. I follow it until it is just a speck on the horizon.

To think of New York - a shiny new world - tall buildings reaching into the sky. I am a bit dazed. It's a dream and I have no reason to believe that it could come true.

I snap back to reality: I am twenty years old, a wife and a mother. My husband is trying to convince me to go to America. Wow, could that dream from long ago be coming true? Was this the chance I had dreamt of that day long ago at the airport? Was this destiny?

Baby Birgit and me

A Leap Of Faith

My husband was a wonderful man whom I dearly loved, who was an idealist and nonconformist. We felt the doubts and criticism of my family. I disappointed them by marrying so young and having a baby before I was 19. Even my old grade school teacher, Frau Jäger, said: *"What a pity - I always thought you would go far, you would make something of yourself."* Her words still sting even after all these years.

Maybe going to America was a chance to prove ourselves. We could live our life without our families watching every step. We would work very hard, live life on our own terms and eventually become deserving of our families' approval and admiration. I heard stories of people who became successful in America. We could do it too. Convinced, I put my concerns into an imaginary box and firmly closed the lid.

"Horst, let's go for it. Let's try it for a year. We can always come back if it doesn't work out."

We decided it would be best for Horst to go first in order to find work and a place to live before Birgit and I followed him. As expected, when he applied for a visa at the American Consulate, he was told he either had to have a job lined up in New York, a sponsor who would vouch for him in the US, or enough money to support himself. He had none of the above. But it wasn't like Horst to give up that easily. He found out that Canada had a much more lenient immigration policy.

He told me *"I'll go to Canada first and then make my way into the US from there."*

As the practical one I asked, "How would you do that? Wouldn't you still have to meet the same requirements for a visa to the US?" Horst the optimist said, *"I will cross that bridge when I come to it."*

Horst was convinced that the place for him was New York, but if it had to be via Canada, so be it. He got his Canadian visa and booked passage on an old converted aircraft carrier "The Seven Seas." On a fine day in May 1960, he was ready to leave, with a few dollars in his pocket and a huge portion of confidence. He went by train from Düsseldorf to Bremerhaven where The Seven Seas was ready for the journey across the Atlantic Ocean to Montreal, Canada. Here are my memories of the day Horst left:

It is close to midnight at the train station in Düsseldorf. The doors to the train are open, departure just a minute away. We hug and kiss, hold each other for a moment longer. "Write soon," I ask through my tears. "I will, I will," Horst says, but I can tell he is already focused on the adventure ahead. He enters the train, the doors close shut with a bang and the train slowly pulls out of the station.

We wave until we lose sight of each other. I notice how cold it is and I shiver.

The huge train station is almost empty. I linger for a while and then slowly make my way home where I crawl into bed and curl up, tears soaking my pillow. When will I see him again, how long will it be? Will he find what he is looking for? Is this the beginning of a better life for our little family or - I suppress a dark thought - WILL I EVER SEE HIM AGAIN?

Birgit is sleeping peacefully nearby with rosy cheeks. I look at her, silently telling her, "Your Papa just left for America. Don't worry, he will send for us as soon as he has a job and a place for us to live. The three of us will begin an exciting new life in the New World."

Waiting For News

Shortly after Horst left, I found a small two-room attic apartment in a four-story walk-up with no heat or water. There was a sink and toilet in between floors that were shared by three families. Far from ideal, but it was a place of my own. Horst's parents agreed to take care of Birgit during the week while I worked at my secretarial job. On weekends, Birgit was with me in our little place. At one and one-half years old, she was too young to miss her Papa for very long. I felt alone and unsure about the future, waiting anxiously for Horst's letters.

Because I needed to feel closer to my husband, I knitted him a wool sweater - black with red patterns. I remember sitting alone in my attic room after work, wrapped in a blanket, knitting and crying. My tears became part of that sweater. When it was finished, I sent it to him and felt a little better, envisioning him wearing it and thinking about me.

He wrote about his adventurous ocean journey and his first impressions of Canada. One of his letters described his journey from Montreal to Toronto and Ottawa to Calgary.

It took him almost five days by train. I almost fell off my chair - FIVE DAYS?!

How could that be? *Where in the world is he?* I looked at a map of America and realized for the first time the immensity of that country. It was unimaginable how far away he was - making me feel even more vulnerable about our future. In

Germany and Europe everything is so close together, one can travel from north to south or from east to west Germany in a single day.

Here I was, 20 years old with a baby and my husband in a far-faraway place. How would it all turn out? However, in all my worry and concern, I never lost a sense of underlying excitement; a feeling of hope and confidence that this was the beginning of a new and better life for us.

I remember feeling envious of my girlfriend Annemarie. While I was a mother with an absent husband, she was going from party to party, dating interesting men, traveling to sunny places and buying a new pair of shoes every month. I had to save whatever I could to have enough for our anticipated passage to America. Even after all these years, I sometimes think about that time and am grateful that I can buy a new pair of shoes - even two - every month if I want to.

Birgit and me in Düsseldorf

One long year had passed since Horst left for New York via Canada. Now our wait was finally over. Birgit and I were on board the ocean liner TS Bremen crossing the Atlantic from Bremerhaven, Germany to New York, where Horst had found a job and an apartment.

May 31, 1961. Our ship is preparing for tomorrow's arrival at New York Harbor. There is a heightened sense of anticipation and excitement among the passengers - our seven-day journey is ending. While I am busy putting Birgit to bed in our cabin, my thoughts rush ahead to tomorrow's arrival. How will it be to see Horst again after an entire year of separation? Will Birgit, now two-and-a-half, recognize her Papa? She was just a baby, a little over a year old, when he left for America. Oh the anticipation is tremendous and so many questions come to mind. What will New York be like? Will I like the apartment Horst rented for us? How will I get along with the few words of English I know? My heart is pounding with an overwhelming feeling of excitement mixed with the fear of the unknown. Sleep is hard to come by on this last night in our tiny cabin.

My thoughts returned to last year at about this time. Horst had left for Canada. In his letters, he kept me up to date about his experiences. His English was good enough to help him navigate daily life. To get by, he had taken whatever jobs he could find, first in Toronto, then in Calgary and Edmonton. His jobs ranged from brick layer to ballroom dance instructor. He realized early on that his dream of working as a photographer had to stay a dream for a while longer.

However, his camera was always with him. He photographed everything around him. Some of those photos are now classics, like the one he took of a bucking horse and rider at the famed Calgary Stampede. It became apparent that Canada was not the place for him to build a career in his chosen field. And as soon as he had saved up enough for a bus ticket, he was on his way to New York, traveling all the way back across the continent. How did he make it across the Canadian border without a US visa? That was a bit sketchy - he still chuckles today when he tells the story. *"I just charmed my way in - I somehow convinced the official at the US Consulate to issue me a visa - I remember he asked me how much money I had. Of course, I only had a few dollars, but I must have made an impression on him as an honest and responsible person. He just issued me the visa."*

When Horst arrived in New York, he had enough money to rent a tiny flat in Manhattan and soon found a job in a photo lab that paid $50 a week. He decided that was enough to support his little family.

He wrote, *"It's time for you to come join me. I have a job and will find a place for us to live. I can't wait to see how Birgit has grown in the year we were apart and whether she remembers me. Finally, we can be together again and start our new life here in the new world."*

The Crossing

While Horst was away, I saved every penny I could and eventually had enough to book the passage from Bremerhaven to New York on the beautiful ocean liner TS Bremen. First, Birgit and I had to travel by train to Frankfurt to apply for a visa at the US Consulate. After hours of interviews, pages of applications (with questions like: are you intending to be a spy? Will you bring illegal drugs with you?), physical exams and several rounds of smallpox vaccinations, we had our visas in our hands.

On May 25, 1961, we said goodbye to family and friends and headed to Bremerhaven, where our ship was waiting at the dock. A good friend of Erhard's drove us there from Düsseldorf. Papi and Mutti and sister Friedel came along to see us off. I remember little of what must have been an emotional farewell, not knowing when we would see each other again.

Once on board, we quickly checked out our tiny cabin before heading up on deck. We searched the many faces on the dock for our loved ones. There they were, scanning the ship's outdoor decks for a glimpse of us. We were standing at the ship's railing on an upper deck and spotted one another. As we waved to each other, the ship emitted an ear-splitting sound from its steam whistle - *booooooom, booooooom, booooooom* - and we started moving ever so slowly away from the pier. A band played the well-known German folk song "muss i denn muss i denn zum Städtele hinaus." The song is about bidding farewell to a loved one and the heartbreak of being left behind. Tears were rolling, handkerchiefs flying in farewell. The tug boats guided the TS Bremen out of the harbor into the open sea for our seven-day crossing.

I was so excited that the enormity of this moment didn't really sink in. My thoughts were racing ahead to seeing my husband again after an entire year apart and starting a brand-new adventure, a new life. Birgit and I settled into our tiny cabin, which we shared with a nice young woman, Fräulein Schmidt.

Our big journey to the NEW WORLD -- AMERICA on board the TS BREMEN May 25 - June 1, 1961

Papi, Friedel, Mutti, Birgit and me

TS Bremen leaving Bremerhaven

Our life on board was very pleasant, with lots of fun activities and excellent food. For me it was the biggest adventure of my lifetime - yet it was just the beginning. Birgit had great fun playing with lots of children in the ship's "Kids Club." At first she didn't want me to leave and started to cry when she noticed I was leaving the room, but after a while she looked forward to being with her new friends and the very nice attendants.

Another brand new experience was passing through different time zones as we crossed the ocean. Six times during our trip we set our clocks back one hour.

On our last night on the Atlantic, we encountered rough seas. The ship was rolling from side to side, making the farewell dance a lot of fun. Couples had to hang onto each other as they slid across the slanting floor, bumping into each other. No one seemed concerned about the turbulent seas. We were just having fun and felt safe - we were almost at our destination. Birgit slept peacefully through it all.

Reunited

Early the next day, June 1, as I looked out of our porthole, there was a sight to behold: The New York skyline. Soon the ship was slowly gliding along what looked like tall concrete walls and unfamiliar looking buildings rising right outside our cabin - I could almost touch them - *we were here, in New York*. With a pounding heart, I gathered Biggi and our bags and headed along the corridor, following the other passengers on their way out of the ship and onto the Pier 88 terminal. There was great chaos with all the people and their trunks, bags and belongings. A very long, slow line formed towards immigration and customs clearance. It was hot and sticky and so difficult for me to wait in this line. I was terribly excited.

I wanted to run ahead and find Horst. Was he here? What if he wasn't? The wait was almost unbearable. Then, all of a sudden, there was an announcement over the loudspeaker: *"Mrs.*

Erika Schafer, please come to the front of the line." Even with my limited English, I knew what that meant. My heart took a big leap, I grabbed Birgit and we pushed our way through the crowds. Horst's new boss, Mr. Schulman, greeted us. He had used his press credentials to get priority processing for us. It didn't take long at all and we were on our way to the exit.

And there he was, hurrying towards us with a big grin on his face, a bouquet of red roses in one hand and a yellow rubber duck in the other. We flew into each other's arms. We held each other for what seemed like a long time until we realized we had almost forgotten little Birgit in the heat of the moment. She stood there, staring at this stranger who was kissing and hugging her Mutti. I had, of course, prepared her: *"Your Papa will meet us when we get off the ship, he is so excited to see you. He will take us to our new home, an apartment just for the three of us and he will take good care of us."* She looked up at him with her big eyes, but there was no recognition on her face. Timidly, with one finger on her lip, she said questioningly, *"Onkel (uncle) Papa?"* We laughed, and he won her over when he handed her the yellow rubber duck. From that moment on she did not leave her Papa's side. We were a family again and very happy at that precious moment.

Reunion at pier 88 New York

Hi – *Uncle?* Papa?

Lady Liberty And Good Humor

My first impressions of New York came while on our taxi ride to Battery Park at the southern tip of Manhattan to get to the ferry and on to Staten Island. Inside the taxi, I glimpsed tall buildings which seemed all jumbled together into a huge mass, the narrow streets hardly visible. I didn't know what to make of it.

Everything looked so foreign, so different. I was impressed and overwhelmed, but also surprised - I envisioned a shiny, modern new world with gleaming chrome and glass buildings. What I saw instead were old-fashioned structures, run-down storefronts and all sorts of people rushing in all directions on the narrow sidewalks.

On the Staten Island Ferry I finally saw her - *the Statue of Liberty* - her right arm raised high in what appeared to be a greeting. What a sight - I had only seen images of her in books and magazines. Now it really sank in - *we are in New York*. Horst treated us to our very first Good Humor ice cream cone on the ferry. It was delicious.

The immigrants with the Statue of Liberty

The ferry docked with a lot of banging and grinding noises. Horst walked us out of the terminal and up the hill, past what looked like government buildings, to our furnished apartment in an old three-story house: 128 Stuyvesant Place. The apartment, while small and old, was a testament to Horst's talent for searching and finding the unconventional, the extraordinary. It was on the first floor of an old Victorian house. It had two rooms and a bathroom. The large room was a combination living room and bedroom. Next to it was the narrow kitchen with a small table and enough room for a bed for Birgit. Our new home had tall ceilings and creaky wooden floors. The bathroom was a bit run down, but it had hot running water and a tub with a shower.

We rejoiced that we now had a place of our own, just for the three of us. I decorated our apartment with the few things I had packed in the one trunk I could bring: linens, candlesticks, vases, books. It didn't take long for us to feel at home. Birgit had no trouble adjusting. She had her Mutti and Papa and several cats who belonged to the other tenants to play with. She endeared herself to our neighbors by handing out little bouquets of dandelions she picked in the front yard. When there were no more flowers, she made do with bunches of grass. One nice gentleman fell in love with her and came by almost every day. Sometimes he would take her to a nearby store and treat her to an ice cream cone (red flag going up in your mind? No worries, we made sure she was safe).

The best thing about that apartment - so special and totally wonderful - was a pair of tall French doors that opened from our living room/bedroom onto the front yard of the house with an unobstructed view between tall buildings on either side, to the New York harbor.

When we looked out through those French doors, even while lying in bed, we could see the big ocean liners slowly making their way into the harbor. Repeatedly we spotted the

Queen Elizabeth, Queen Mary, SS France and many other ships from all over the world, including "our" TS Bremen. As these magnificent ships slowly moved out of our sight, they announced their arrival into the harbor with the deep booming blasts from their steam whistles. I still get goosebumps remembering this.

Those first days and weeks were filled with all kinds of discoveries. There were so many new impressions. Most of it I embraced with enthusiasm and excitement. However, the cockroaches in our apartment took some getting used to. Back home, cockroaches were a sign of living in filth and poverty. Even though my family lived modestly, the idea of pests in our home was unthinkable.

It surprised me how old-fashioned most buildings looked. In my imagination everything in the new world was steel and glass, shiny and modern. Even people's homes were furnished with what looked to me like old stuff. I learned later that oftentimes these items were valuable and treasured antiques. In Germany, most of the "old stuff" had been destroyed in the war and replaced with modern products, sleek in design and attractive in their simplicity. No one wanted old ornate things any more.

When it was time to do our little family's first laundry, I knew what I needed: a very large pot to boil our whites the way I was used to. Horst knew where to go, a hardware store. *"You want what?"* the salesperson said, giving us a strange look. "Well, you know, a big pot for boiling laundry," Horst explained. Another strange look, then a shrug of the shoulders - obviously American housewives had other ways of doing their wash - laundromats. I was appalled. "How can you get your sheets and underwear clean if they are not boiled?"

But we adapted and Birgit and I spent many hours in the laundromat in our neighborhood. While waiting for the dryer to finish, we discovered Butterfingers in the vending machine and they became a favorite treat.

Horst brought home about $45 a week after taxes. Our rent was $72 per month. Since we never had $72 at once, we paid the rent weekly out of his paycheck, leaving $27 for everything else. Although we must have been below the poverty line, we didn't feel poor. The resourcefulness I learned from my Mutti came in handy to make every penny count. Sure, we had no car, no phone, no radio or TV or any of the other common conveniences of that time, but we just optimistically made the most of what we had.

We explored the wonders of New York and its surroundings to our heart's content at very little cost - ferry, subway and bus fares were a nickel each and kids were free. Most of the museums, zoos, botanical gardens, and beaches were free. Equipped with picnic food for the entire day, we would leave early in the morning on weekends, crisscrossing New York City and its suburbs on the vast subway and bus system. Returning late at night, we were tired but exhilarated by all we had seen and experienced. We saw more of New York in those first few months than most people see in a lifetime. And all on less than $2 a day.

Hermann and Bubi

One day as we were walking around Central Park, we saw a baby squirrel lying helplessly on the ground below a big tree. It had fallen out of its nest. We waited to see if the parents would come and help it back up the tree, but nothing happened. We couldn't just leave it to be taken by a large bird or other predator. Horst picked it up and tucked the frightened baby squirrel inside his shirt. That's where it stayed the entire way home, first on the subway, then the ferry.

We called him Hermann, and he became our pet with free rein in the apartment. Soon all three of us had lots of tiny scratches from Hermann climbing all over us. It wasn't long before we realized it wasn't a good idea to keep a wild animal as a pet. Horst put Hermann in a cage and took him to a zoo where he released him.

Birgit with Hermann

Another time we rescued a baby starling that had fallen out of its nest. We called him Bubi and fed him soft cat food until he started to fly. He was so tame that when we let him fly outside he had no fear of neighbor cats who lay in wait. He even would come flying home when we called his name. Again, it became too stressful to have him fly (and poop) all over the house. We tried a big birdcage, but he almost broke his wings trying to get out. Our landlords owned a cabin in the woods. One day they took Bubi with them and released him in the forest.

What Were You Thinking?

Most of the time I felt confident and full of hope for our future, but there was one day that is etched in my memory when the reality of our situation came crashing down on me.

Horst usually came home from work on the ferry around dinner time. On that day, dinner went by without a sign of him. It became dark, then 9, 10, 11 p.m. and no sign of him. A terrible worry came over me, a dark foreboding. What if something happened to him in the vast stone canyons of Manhattan? How would I find him? Who could I contact? We had no phone, so he could not call me and I could not call him. I did not know where he was or who he was with. What if he just disappeared? Or got mugged or, worse, killed?

An immense wave of dread and terror grabbed me. I broke out in a cold sweat and my heart beat wildly. I felt intensely alone and helpless. What would I do if he never came home?

Suddenly, in a matter of hours, our life here that felt so exciting, so full of hope and promise, had turned into a hostile and threatening nightmare. I only felt a little better when my mind created a "relief valve." Should my worst fears come true, I knew with certainty what I would do: I would take Birgit and go home - yes, home to my family in Germany. I would find a way. Home - that comforting thought helped me calm down a bit.

But it was driving me mad to just sit around the apartment, so in my desperation I walked down to the ferry terminal in the middle of the night, leaving Birgit asleep in her bed. The huge ferry building was dark and deserted. Not a soul anywhere. Too frantic to be worried about my own safety, I waited till the next ferry arrived - the few departing passengers rushed past me and did not include my husband. My fear deepened, and I wanted to wait for the next boat, but I remembered Birgit alone in the apartment and I returned with a heavy heart.

Then, finally, at two a.m. the door opened and Horst walked in. "*What are you doing up at this hour?*" he said casually. I could hardly talk. I was so filled with a combination of enormous relief and great fury. "*Where were you, didn't you know how worried I would be?*" He looked surprised and said:

"I was with a friend and the time just got away from me." All I could think was "*** *MEN!* ***" The relief of having my world restored was so great that I don't remember staying mad at him for long.

Billy Ball And Peter Pim

I only spoke a few words of English when I arrived, but somehow I found my way - pointing and smiling - I picked up the language gradually. Horst had learned English in school and could communicate well. The little I knew I had learned in Frau Jäger's grade school class.

She had lived in England for a few years and offered interested students weekly lessons after school. One of those early lessons went like this: *"Billy Ball, short and small, cannot have a heavy fall. But his chum, Peter Pim, is a lad long and slim."* That didn't get me very far in New York, but things improved when I enrolled in an English class at a nearby High School.

While it was nice that the owners of the house we lived in were German, it didn't help me much with learning English. A year after arriving, I found a part-time job with a German travel agency which didn't help much either since most of their clients were Germans who wanted to converse in their native tongue. Only when we moved to Bayside, Queens, in 1963 did I make big strides.

While adjusting to American cuisine wasn't that difficult, we yearned for some foods we were used to. To our delight we discovered York Town, a German immigrant neighborhood on 86th Street in Manhattan. There we found lots of familiar foods imported from home - breads, sausages, cold cuts, sauerkraut, pastries and many other specialties. Soon a weekly trip to York Town became part of our routine.

We moved to Bayside in 1963 after finding out we were expecting an addition to our little family. Our Staten Island apartment was too small for a family of four. Horst had landed a great new job around that time. The New York Racing Association, which operated the famed Aqueduct and Belmont horse racing tracks, hired him as on-site photographer. His job was to photograph the daily training activities around the paddock. He was well paid, which allowed us to move, buy a car - an old Oldsmobile - and furnish an apartment. And we finally had a telephone. My special joy was a brand-new Telefunken stereo. I discovered that each Saturday there were live broadcasts by the Metropolitan Opera. I, of course, became a regular listener.

Again, Horst had found a great new place for us to live, a two-bedroom unit in a garden apartment complex in Bayside, Queens. Rows of two-story buildings were situated around a large, open courtyard. Our neighbors were mostly young families with children. The kids had plenty of friends and a safe place to play. It was ideal for us - total immersion in the American way of life. No German spoken here. It forced Birgit and me to speak English which we picked up quickly.

Biggi had lots of new friends and I became acquainted with several of the mothers. Our apartment was on the ground floor. Above us lived a lovely couple with two small daughters - the Bouchards. We became good friends and did many things together, including almost nightly rounds of scrabble when the kids were sleeping.

Memories of a summer night in Bayside: Click, click, click - continuous clicking sounds woke me up from my drowsy sleep. I was lying hot and sweaty on damp bed sheets - summer in New York with daytime temperatures of 98 degrees in the shade and 90% humidity with little relief at night, there was no air conditioning. The clicking came from outside our apartment. Some neighbors were still playing croquet at midnight. Instead of tossing and turning in the stifling heat in their homes, they preferred to catch whatever nightly breeze might kick up outside. Many a night, Horst was among them. I preferred to take a cold shower just before going to bed, then lying down dripping wet with a wet washcloth wrapped around my neck - hoping to fall asleep before the cooling effect of the wet cloth wore off.

Heidi Arrives

We experienced a big culture shock when Horst took me to my first doctor's appointment for a pregnancy checkup. Dr. Podolsky, my nice obstetrician, said "*My fee will be $250.00 and the hospital will charge about the same.*" We were speechless. We'd have to pay to have a baby? We had been used to national health care in Germany where you never see a medical bill from the time you are born until you die. Heidi was born on June 12, 1963. It felt really strange when Horst had to "bail us out" so to speak when he came to pick us up from the hospital.

In Germany, besides free healthcare, mothers-to-be who were working got four weeks off before and after delivery with full pay, plus a daily allowance for nursing. How naïve we were to expect something like that in the US. But we were fortunate that Horst was making good money now, and we could save enough for our new arrival.

Another culture shock: American mothers thought breastfeeding was, let's say, "backwards." Their babies were bottle fed from the day they were born.

As much as I embraced the American ways, that seemed absurd to me and I insisted on feeding Heidi the old-fashioned way. While at the hospital, I remember a young mother in the bed next to me, her breasts tightly bound to suppress the milk flow - she was in terrible pain. How ridiculous was that? Sticking to my guns, I got a few strange looks, but I was convinced that what I was doing was what nature intended and that it was good for my baby and me.

122

Baby Heidi

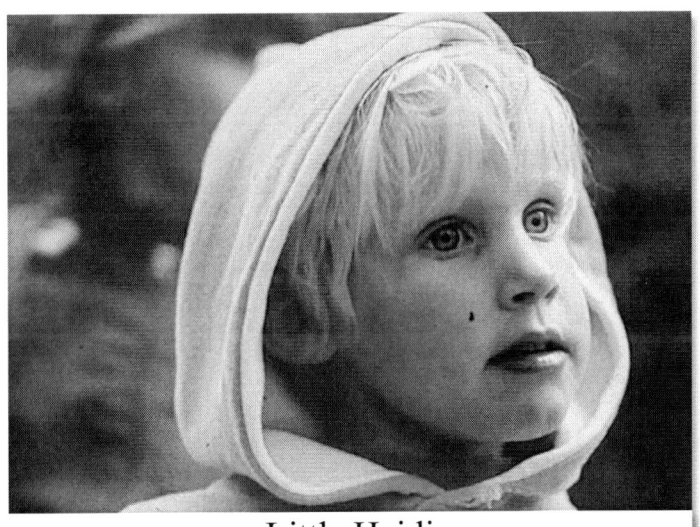

Little Heidi

First Trip Back To Germany

During those early years I don't remember being homesick, however I often wondered how long it would be before we could afford a trip home to visit our families. Letters flowed back and forth every week, but how lovely it would be to see them again. I wanted to tell them in person about our new life. While we still lived on Staten Island, I inquired about the price of airline tickets and did some calculating: assuming we could save a quarter every day, how long would it take? Airline tickets were about $500, times three makes $1,500, divided by 25 cents per day makes - what? - 15 years. FIFTEEN YEARS! Everything in me rebelled and all I could think was *"There's got to be another way!"* I went into denial and put that horrible thought out of my mind.

Thankfully, shortly after we moved to Bayside we were on a plane headed home for a visit. We saved enough for a trip home thanks to Horst's well paying job and a bonus he received. We left Kennedy Airport in December 1963, Birgit was five years old and Heidi six months. Our flight was with Icelandic Airlines in a turboprop machine - 18 hours from New York to Reykjavik, Iceland and then another three hours to Luxembourg.

I will never forget stepping out of the plane upon arrival and seeing my brother Horst and other family members waving to us from the terminal. We fell into each other's arms, all of us talking at the same time. Soon the girls were the center of attention. *"Birgit has grown so much - look how adorable baby Heidi is."* It took another four hours of driving to get to Düsseldorf and my parents' home. It felt good to be home again after being away for over three years.

Everything looked so much smaller to us, life seemed slower, and many of the familiar places and people looked strange to us, but it didn't take long for us to feel at home again.

When it was time for us to go back to New York, it wasn't as sad as the first time.

We felt good about our new life and were confident we would visit again. Hugging goodbye we said "maybe some of you can come visit us in New York" - a very happy thought.

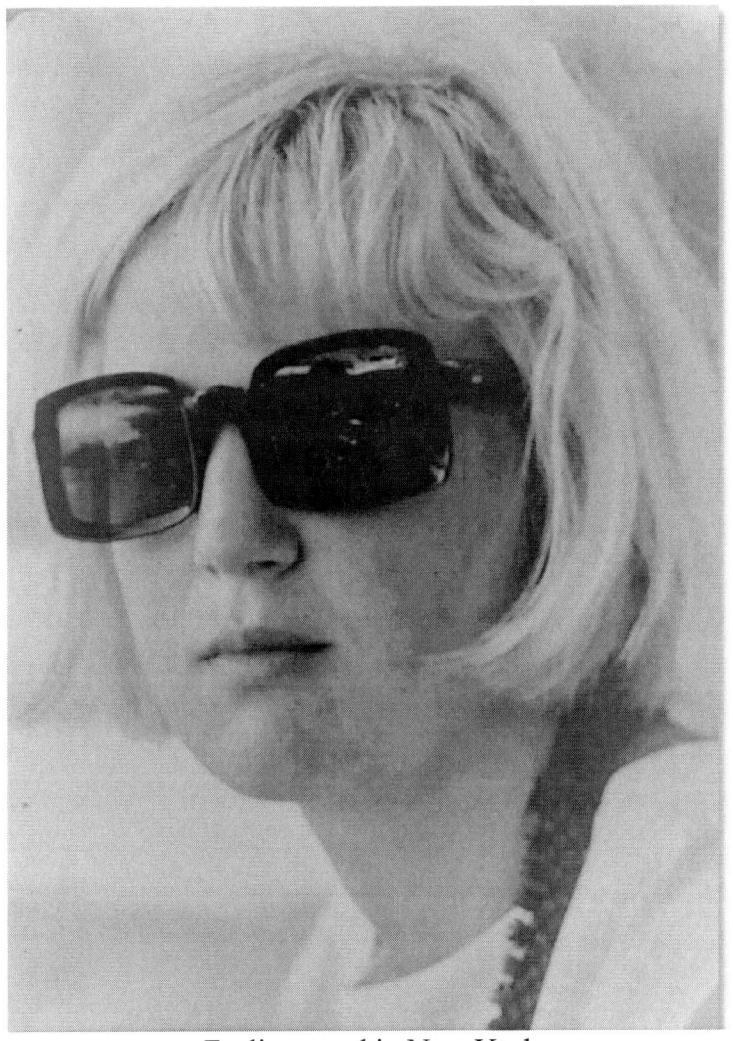

Feeling good in New York

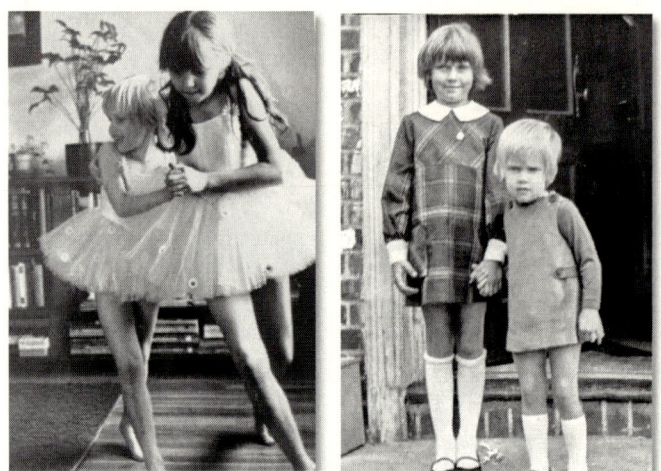

Sisters Birgit and Heidi in New York and…..

…in Dirndl dresses in Germany.

We were happy living in Bayside for four years until we heard rumors of a change in ownership of the garden apartment complex, possibly foreshadowing undesirable changes and higher rents. That drove our decision to move again in 1967. As before, Horst wouldn't just settle for any ordinary apartment - it had to be special. He wanted room for the kids to play and explore outside, which was not a simple task in New York City. After a long search, he said one day, "*I found the perfect place, come and look.*" He took us to Flushing, Queens.

Apartment #54-19 was in a row of modest red brick townhomes on 151st Street. An exterior stair led to our second-floor unit. There was a small eat-in kitchen, a comfortable living room, two bedrooms and one bathroom. The small backyard had a very large weeping willow tree with a swing for our girls. Best of all, across the street was a community soccer field and other green spaces, perfect for all kinds of fun activities for Birgit and Heidi, then ages nine and four, and their new friends.

The girls shared the smaller of the two bedrooms. We bought them brand new bunk beds and Horst custom made bright yellow and orange desks for them. A back door from their bedroom led outside onto a raised wooden deck with stairs to the yard below. Climbing that willow tree became one of their favorite activities.

Ballet And High Heels

Birgit had a passion for dancing. She constantly danced around the house, with and without music. Her movements were creative and carried out with great enthusiasm, her face serious and intent. As for props, she used whatever she found around the house - scarves, small blankets, pieces of fabric.

We felt she was ready for dance lessons and enrolled both girls in a private modern dance school run by an energetic woman from eastern Europe. Mrs. Benoff loved teaching Birgit and told us that she had real talent. Heidi worked to contort her body to emulate her big sister. Birgit loved to perform in front of anyone willing to watch. Her favorite dance music was "Swan Lake" to which she performed whenever we had visitors.

Heidi was more interested in athletic and domestic ambitions. One day she decided to be a Mommy. She put on my high heels and went shopping. That's pretty typical for little girls, except she snuck out of the house and went missing. I was frantic with worry. Where could she be? Few things are as frightening as a missing child. To my immense relief, a neighbor soon brought her home. Heidi had taken her shopping trip seriously and headed for the nearby supermarket - in my high heels. She was just about to cross a busy street when our neighbor recognized her and brought her home.

Heidi on an adventure

Hiking in upstate New York

Birgit, Heidi and me in Flushing, N.Y.

ASSORTED MEMORIES

Our life took shape

In New York ... our new home

We had hoped for a new beginning

had taken the chance

And we had found it

Our future here was full of promise

Thank you New York

For opening the doors for us

It was 1968, seven years after we came to New York, when to our great joy and excitement, my parents were en route from Düsseldorf to visit us. We missed each other so much.

This was their first time so far away from home - the trip of a lifetime for them - and a chance for us to show off our life in New York. There was so much we wanted to show them. On this fine summer day, our wait was finally over. With high anticipation, the four of us were standing on the observation deck at New York's Kennedy International Airport. From where we stood, we watched their World Airways flight land and slowly taxi to the terminal. We quickly ran inside the terminal to a place where we could overlook the baggage claim area on the floor below. First, they had to make their way through customs and immigration. We waited impatiently until we saw them walking toward the exit doors. There were hugs, kisses and happy tears before we headed to our apartment in Flushing. We arranged that Mutti and Papi would sleep in the master bedroom. Horst and I would sleep on the couch in the living room.

Birgit and Heidi, then 10 and 5, were so excited to have their Oma and Opa around. Luckily, Horst always insisted we speak German at home, so they had no problem communicating with their grandparents. We couldn't wait to show them around our new world, but first they needed a day to just settle in. When they were ready, we drove them all over the city.

The sights and sounds of New York totally overwhelmed them and they took it all in enthusiastically, the good and the not-so-good of life in New York. Their necks were stiff from looking up at the dizzying heights of the Manhattan skyscrapers.

They were in awe of the rushing crowds in the streets, the sea of honking cars and streams of yellow taxicabs, noisy subway cars screeching, the constant low rumble that forms the background sound of life in Manhattan.

Craning our necks looking up at the skyscrapers

I was so proud and happy to show them how exciting our life was in this new world. There are two especially fond memories of their visit which are:

Chinese Chicken

On this day - a typical hot and sticky summer day in New York - I am taking my parents to Chinatown. We arrive by subway and are in a totally different world for them - narrow streets lined with many shops displaying weird and sometimes repulsive things such as plucked chickens and ducks with their heads still attached and tongues hanging out, strung up by their necks in store windows. We see large, colorful signs in Chinese everywhere, dirty and narrow sidewalks, Asian people of all kinds rushing in all directions, looking serious and intent.

"What about something to eat?" asks Papi. We had developed a good appetite for lunch. There are, of course, restaurants galore, but which one should we try? I remember someone telling me to look for a place that appears to be a true neighborhood restaurant rather than the ones catering to tourists. I was told, if the locals are there, you can have a true ethnic experience. We spot such a place in the lower level of an old building. We are timid going down the well-worn steps. On entering we have some doubts - it is dark and grimy. The few tables are occupied by busily chatting Chinese people - no English spoken anywhere.

We remember why we chose this local restaurant and bravely sit down at an empty table in a dark corner. We relax and are actually proud of ourselves to have found this place. Our server who, of course, doesn't speak a word of English (never mind German), hands us the menu-everything is in Chinese with no translations. We do not know what we are looking at and feel helpless. "Maybe this wasn't such a good idea after all," I say to myself. Unsure, I point to one of the menu items and look questioningly at our friendly waiter. He thinks for a moment, then smiles and flaps his bent arms up and down. "Oh, chicken," I say with relief. I smile at him, point at the "chicken" on the menu, nodding with emphasis, hold up three fingers and nod some more. What can be so bad about chicken, right? We relax and wait for our lunch. It arrives in no time. The server puts the three plates in front of us. I wish I had a photo of our faces. Proudly sitting in the middle of each plate are three dark, leathery duck feet with legs attached, sticking straight up, all sitting in a brownish liquid - smoked duck feet. Oh my - we said nothing for a while - what do we do now?

My brave and usually not so adventurous father slowly raises a duck foot to his nose, smells it, and takes a tiny bite. He smiles at us in surprise, "Nicht schlecht (not bad)," which is our clue to follow his example.

They are really delicious, smoky, and tender, and the sauce is yummy. We finish every bite. The waiter, who has been watching us out of the corner of his eye, pretends nothing out of the ordinary has happened when he gives us our bill. After paying, we get up and have a hard time making it out of the restaurant before cracking up and laughing all the way to the subway station.

Smoked duck feet made an otherwise ordinary lunch memorable to this day- over fifty years after it happened. I still get a smile on my face when I remember that day.

Grand Opera

As mentioned in an earlier story, it was Mutti who made me a fan of opera. She was an enthusiastic opera lover with season tickets to the Düsseldorf Opera. It was a special treat for her to dress up for a performance. Papi was not an opera buff. He preferred to stay home when Mutti and cousin Wolfgang went together to an opera in Düsseldorf.

Before my parents arrived in New York, an idea had formed in my mind: What if I could take Mutti and Papi to the

New York Metropolitan Opera? What if they could experience a performance in one of the world's best opera houses? The idea took hold of me and before too long I took the subway to Manhattan and stood in line at the box office of the Met. The popular opera "Aida" by Giuseppe Verdi was playing. When I saw the ticket prices - good seats were $17.00 each - I had to swallow hard. Yikes, that's $51.00 for the three of us! A small fortune.

Money was still tight, and I wondered how I could justify spending that much on tickets. Can I be that frivolous? I was still contemplating when it became my turn at the box office window, so I let some other people ahead of me. I needed a few more minutes to decide. *Should I do it?*

Deep down, I knew I had to go for it. It would be an experience of a lifetime for the three of us.

So I bravely handed $51.00 to the ticket clerk and held the three tickets in my hand. Yes, it was the right thing to do; I was certain of it.

The night of the performance was truly magical. Few experiences in my life have brought me so much happiness as this monumentally epic performance inside the glorious Metropolitan Opera with my Mutti and Papi. What an incredible treat to hear some of the world's most famous opera stars, Grace Bumbry as Aida, Carlo Bergonzi as Radames.

As I watched, Papi (not really an opera fan), became mesmerized with the multitude of trumpet players high above the stage during the triumphal scene. Well over one hundred performers were on stage during that scene, including an elephant. The glorious music touched us deeply and gladdened our souls - w*hat a beautiful experience.* To this day I feel so grateful I had this amazing time with my parents.

Over the years in New York, we had other visitors from the old country. Horst's parents, Alma and Max Schäfer, made the journey. So did my then 15-year-old brother Willi and my dear friend Annemarie. We never tired of showing them around and delighting in their glee at being in New York.

My parents in New York

At Aqueduct horse race track

It's early morning in Flushing in the summer of 1969 with not a cloud in the sky. It promises to be a glorious day, perfect for a day in the park. Horst looks out our living room window: "They are here, are we ready?" I panic, "Just give me a moment, I'm finishing the last batch of pancakes." The girls are still half asleep and grumpy from being woken up so early. Horst says with impatience: "Come on, let's go, they are waiting for us."

Finally, we are ready. My face is still hot from bending over the stove. Let's see, 13 people at three pancakes each, that's 39 pancakes. No wonder I wasn't ready in time. The four of us run down the front stairs to meet our friends who are waiting in their cars. Soon our little caravan of four families in four cars, packed with people and supplies is headed north, away from the city to our favorite picnic spot: Ward Pound Ridge State Park in Westchester County. We have enough provisions to spend the entire day in the park: that large batch of special pancakes for breakfast (thin crepes rolled up with Lingonberries and sprinkled with powdered sugar) as well as blankets, ropes for swinging on trees, croquet sets, jump ropes, balls, and badminton sets.

We stored food for lunch and dinner in coolers. The plan was to spend the entire day in the park and drive home after dinner to avoid the infamous traffic jams back into the city. Horst instigated most of our outings. He insisted we leave the hectic city behind on weekends and enjoy the beautiful countryside around New York.

Pound Ridge was a vast park with amazing natural settings and picnic areas.

Having fun at Pound Ridge park

Our Immigrant Group

Our group was comprised of four families - all recent immigrants. We quickly became friends.

There were Theo and Renate Frobin, both from Berlin with their children Michael and Angela, about the same age as our girls. Theo worked for Lufthansa Airlines. Then there were Peter and Helena Pedross and their young son Jan. Peter was from the Tyrol region of Germany and also worked for Lufthansa. Helena grew up in Finland. The fourth couple were Rolf and Alice Kohnert. Rolf, a Viking of a man, was a carpenter from Bremen and his petite wife Alice was from Switzerland. They had no children yet although later they had a little girl.

Our group of eight adults and five children became inseparable; we were each other's ersatz (substitute) families. The children were like cousins. We spent most weekends together. We had a major goal in common: we wanted to make it in America; we wanted to experience the American Dream in the land of unlimited opportunity. Still living hand-to-mouth, we shared great hopes and dreams of making it, each couple in a different way. Horst wanted to be successful as a fine-art photographer, Peter wanted to make it big in business, Theo saw a big future for himself within Lufthansa Airlines, and Rolf and Alice just wanted to have a normal life without grand ambitions.

Every Saturday our group gathered for impromptu parties at each other's houses, most often at our apartment in Flushing. We cooked and ate together, then put the kids to bed, all in one room, and got out the wine and put on dance music. The cheapest wine we could find was Gallo Rhine Garten.

It came in gallon bottles - we emptied plenty of them. We danced to the new dance sensation—the Twist—and listened to The Beatles and Chubby Checker. We contorted our bodies into pretzels playing "Twister" and competed at "Limbo" -- "How low can you go?"

Wildwood Beach

"Look, they are being carried out into the bay, we need to get help fast." One of our biggest adventures is also one that almost turned tragic.

We went on a camping weekend to a remote beach at Wildwood Beach State Park on the north shore of Long Island Sound. Horst and Theo had scouted the area and picked a spot far away from the public beaches, a stretch of beautiful isolated beaches, accessible only by scrambling down steep, thirty-foot high sand dunes.

We loaded our cars with everything we needed for six adults and five children. There were no services or amenities at this beach, so everything had to be brought in, including toilet paper, blankets, sheets, flash lights and enough food and drink.

We arrived at the site and looked down the steep slope. Oh my, how are we going to get all that gear down there? We tested it out by running and hopping down in the soft sand. It was a blast - with each step we sank deep into the sand, sliding downward, squealing with laughter and delight as we were trying to keep our balance. It was a hoot. The kids especially had a blast. We all got into the act, hopping, running, sliding - we must have looked like a bunch of grasshoppers invading the beach. Making it down there with all our gear and supplies was another matter. We had to make several trips. There were a few spills with lots of laughs and teasing, but finally everything was on the beach. No one wanted to talk about how in the world we would get everything back up there again. Let's think about that when the time comes.

We had a lot of work to do, setting up makeshift tents from driftwood, old sheets and rope. We needed two tents, one for the adults and one for the kids. Theo took on the role of master builder and inventor. He scoured the beach for driftwood planks, sticks and tree trunks. He even built tables and benches and a makeshift outhouse. He used long wooden poles and sheets as sun screens. A fire pit completed our "homestead" and all were quite satisfied. The children were in seventh heaven playing in the surf, building sand castles and forts from driftwood, and collecting treasures.

Gallons Of Gallo

As the sun set, we cooked our first dinner in the fire pit: hot dogs, burgers and chicken. We were now ready for a bonfire and some Gallo Rhine Garten. We made sure that we had plenty of gallon-size bottles so as not to run out. It was hot and earlier in the day we had buried the bottles in the wet sand at the water's edge to keep them cool. Now, hours later, we looked and looked, but there was no sign of them near the churning surf — what we hadn't expected was that while we were busy setting up, the tide had come in and covered everything up. Someone yelled "All men aboard" and we all dove into the surf, digging in the sand until we had recovered all the bottles.

Wine never tasted so good.

The next day was sunny and hot, not a cloud in the sky. We relaxed on the beach and took a dip in the water from time to time to cool off. The children didn't need us; they were busy having a wonderful time. Horst had to leave us for a few hours to work at the racetrack. Someone had brought a small inflatable row boat. While most of us were passed out with a hangover on blankets, Peter and Renate did a little rowing. The water was calm and the sky as blue as can be. We watched them as they got into the little boat and leisurely drifted on the calm water. I swam out a ways, passed by their boat and we exchanged a few words. I floated on my back for a while.

When I swam back to shore, I noticed I wasn't making much headway. I was swimming in place instead of toward shore. I was a little alarmed, but finally gained ground and swam back to the beach. I mentioned the odd sensation I had to the others, but no one took it seriously. We lazed in the sun, from time to time watching the little boat with Peter and Renate bobbing in the distance.

Adrift At Sea

After what seemed like hours, someone said, *"Those two are having a great time out there, but shouldn't they be thinking about heading back?"* No one was alarmed, though. Another hour passed. *"Look, they are going out farther and farther."* Finally, it sank in and we jumped to our feet in alarm: *"Are they in trouble? Why can't they make it back to shore?"* Renate's husband Theo yelled *"Look, they are being carried out into the bay, we need to get help fast."* Where to go? We were in such a remote area. Where is the nearest town? We had no phones. Theo started running, scrambling up the steep slope as fast as he could. No one was laughing this time. He jumped into his car, drove to the nearest town, and alerted the Coast Guard.

We were all holding our breath - will they be ok? Will help be coming? The wait was excruciating. Then we heard the droning sound of an approaching helicopter. With relief, we watched from the beach as it circled a few times in the far distance. By now our two friends were a mere speck on the horizon. *Why are they circling, can't they find them*? Finally, the helicopter dipped and what looked like a rope ladder was lowered to the water. We could barely see what was happening because it was so far out, but the two specks who were climbing up the ladder and into the hovering helicopter were Renate and Peter. Thank God, they were safe.

Badly shaken, we couldn't believe what had just happened.

On board the helicopter, Peter and Renate were shivering uncontrollably from exposure. Quickly they were wrapped in blankets and given hot drinks. Later they told us a strong current had pulled them into the deep water. The temperature had dropped dramatically and tall waves had crashed into their flimsy little boat. They lost the oars and could only hang onto the rubber boat for dear life as the waves washed over them. They were so very cold and thought they would not make it. Hypothermia was setting in. They were still shaking and shivering hours after we all got back to the beach. When Horst joined us after work, he was shocked to hear what had happened. It was a huge wake-up call for all of us.

We were so shaken and mortified that we could have lost our friends without realizing they were in trouble. We learned to never underestimate the power and danger of the ocean. While the rest of us were lounging in the sun, being baked under a cloudless sky, our friends had been fighting for their lives. That night on the beach, the Gallo Rhine Garten tasted oh so lovely. We were so grateful to the US Coast Guard who, with their quick action, saved our friends' lives.

The next day we were still a bit dazed. None of us had slept well. Towards afternoon we disassembled our camp and packed up. We were ready to head home. Looking up from the beach, we could see our cars parked over thirty feet above us on top of the dunes. How are we going to get all our stuff up there? Coming down was easy, but going up meant sinking into the sand with every step. How would we do it weighed down with boxes, bags, coolers and all the other stuff?

The men put their heads together and came up with a brilliant solution: They tied a long rope to the front bumper of one of the cars, a rope long enough to reach the beach. Loaded up with as much as we could carry, we took turns grabbing hold of the end of the rope and wrapping it tightly around our wrist. When we gave the signal, the car slowly, carefully backed up, pulling us up, step by step, to the top of the steep slope. When we discovered how well it worked, we made a game of it. Even the children got into the act and couldn't get enough of it. After the last haul, we looked down — there was no sign that anyone had camped down there, except the remnants of the fire pit. Our return home was somber. It could have ended in a great tragedy. How fortunate we were.

David And Georgette

Shortly after coming to New York, Horst met David Preston, also a photographer. They had much in common as photographers and shared their experiences. Horst benefitted from David's knowledge and connections and his willingness to help Horst find his way. David and Georgette, his wife, took us under their wing and we became wonderful friends. They lived in an apartment in Manhattan.

I remember the first time they invited us to dinner; I was so impressed with Georgette's gracious hospitality. She made a delicious meal for us in her tiny kitchen. I watched and admired her skilled handling of the meal preparation. Her parents were Greek immigrants and the meal she prepared reflected the tastes and techniques of her heritage.

At the time, I had picked up little English and therefore was mostly silent during our visit. However, I asked for Georgette's recipe and it is one of my favorite dishes to this day.

Marinated Flank Steak:

1 Flank steak
1 bunch scallions, chopped
½ c chopped parsley
½ c Kikkoman soy sauce
¼ c olive oil
¼ c red wine vinegar
Salt, pepper, oregano

Mix all ingredients and pour over flank steak, marinate for about 24 hours, bake at 375 degrees for 30 minutes. Let sit for 15 minutes and slice very thinly on the diagonal.

_____

Serve with Rice Pilaf:

1 c long grain white rice
2 TS butter
salt, pepper, oregano
2 c chicken broth

Sauté rice in butter until lightly browned, add spices and broth, bring to a boil and cover tightly (a folded kitchen towel under the lid keeps the rice moist and fluffy). Cook over low heat for about 25 minutes.

When Birgit was eight years old, David and Georgette invited her to see The Nutcracker Ballet at Lincoln Center, performed by the New York City Ballet. She felt grown up and special in the velvet dress I made for her and totally loved it. We were grateful to our friends for introducing Biggi to this special holiday treat.

Thus a tradition was born. Almost every Christmas thereafter the girls and I dressed up in our finest dresses and went by bus and subway into Manhattan for the ballet.

After we moved to Denver in 1974 we continued the tradition, first the three of us, then adding, one after another, my eight grandchildren as soon as they were old enough to enjoy the performance, at first sitting on laps or booster seats until they were tall enough to see the stage without help.

After the performance they were treated to their very own wooden nutcrackers.

I jokingly say that over the years I have seen the Nutcracker 475 times - well it just seems that way. I never stopped being enchanted by Tchaikovsky's music and the beautiful ballet and seeing the enchanted faces of my girls and the grandchildren. Thank you, David and Georgette for your gracious and generous friendship.

Birgit the dancer

I enjoyed being a stay-at-home Mom but longed to contribute and help make ends meet, but my English wasn't good enough to find a job. So I focused on something else I was good at: sewing. I learned it from my Mutti, who was a skilled seamstress. She made most of my and my sister Friedel's clothes plus matching outfits for our dolls. Before going to America, I had become proficient in sewing my own dresses.

Our first major purchase after furnishing our apartment was a sewing machine. I insisted on buying the best model on the market - a Singer. Mutti had a Singer, and that's what I wanted. Horst took me shopping, and we came home with a brand new Singer sewing machine, complete with a matching sewing basket, the kind that has pull-out compartments for all the many sewing notions, threads, needles, buttons and so on. I was so happy and made clothes for us girls right away.

I needed to find a good source for fabrics that were of excellent quality but reasonably priced. What I found in the local department stores was disappointing: cheap, garish, and not the quality or style I was looking for. As always when I faced a hurdle, I told myself, *"There's got to be another way."*

Someone told me about the Garment District in Manhattan where I could find good quality fabric remnants really cheap. That's where I needed to go. Arriving by bus and subway somewhere north of West 34th Street, I was initially overwhelmed by the hustle and bustle inside and outside of several old grey 6-story warehouse-type buildings. People with clothes racks on wheels with garments of all kinds were moving hurriedly among the ugly buildings. The entire scene was like a beehive - comings and goings everywhere. Everyone seemed to know where they were headed, except me.

Where should I start and how would I know where to find what I was looking for? I took a deep breath and walked into the nearest building. It was dark and smelly inside. Freight elevators connected several stories of open floors. I saw every imaginable merchandise from fabrics to partially made clothing to sewing notions, buttons, ribbons, lace. The chaos totally overwhelmed me so I bought nothing that first time. But I gathered my courage and soon went back. Walking around with purpose and determination, I found great bargains. My sewing machine started humming and my girls and I had new things to wear.

On one of my trips to the Garment District I met a nice man in his late 50s. He had a big black leather trunk on wheels, which he was loading up with fabric remnants. *"Hi, my name is Hymie. Can I help you with anything?"* He asked, wanting to know what I was doing at the Garment District. I obviously must have looked a bit out of place.

We talked for a while and I don't remember clearly how it came about, but before long Hymie and his trunk on wheels were visiting me in Flushing. He would load up his trunk early in the morning at the Garment District, take two subways and a bus, then walk almost a mile to our apartment. I invited him for breakfast, then checked out what he had in his trunk and was very pleased. It was just what I was looking for, quality fabrics at bargain prices. After that first time, Hymie showed up on many Saturday mornings. Why did he make that long trek? Obviously not just to sell a few scraps of fabric. It turned out that he looked forward to those hearty German breakfasts. He loved the many varieties of cold cuts, different cheeses, sweet butter, plum jam and especially the dark rye bread, which I regularly bought at a nearby German delicatessen.

After walking up the stairs to our apartment, Hymie would put his trunk in a corner and sit down with us, ate with a good appetite, and the three of us enjoyed visiting about life and all kinds of topics. I'd encourage him, *"have another slice of bread, Hymie, and try this delicious blood sausage."*

He was easily convinced: *"Everything tastes so good, how can I refuse?"*

When the breakfast table was cleared, Hymie would open his worn leather trunk and slowly bring out a treasure trove of fabrics. I never knew what would be in that trunk. Sometimes I worried a little. How would I handle it if I didn't like anything? He came such a long way, and I didn't want to disappoint him. Luckily, that never happened. There was always something I liked and I could be certain that everything he had was of excellent quality - colorful cottons, crisp linens, sumptuous woolens and elegant gabardines, sometimes even gorgeous silks and velvets.

There was only one thing: I couldn't ask him for two yards of this and three yards of that. It was the whole bolt or nothing. Most times I ended up with a stack of fabrics that kept me busy for weeks. Often, I had much more of a particular fabric than I needed for one dress (we mostly wore dresses in those days). So, in order to avoid wasting anything, my girls and I often walked around in outfits made from the same fabric, a little like Maria and the children in The Sound of Music. One time I got a little carried away - the girls looked like easter eggs in their bright orange dresses with matching coats and bonnets.

Thanks to Hymie and my Singer sewing machine, it was years before I bought any ready-made clothes for us. The exception, of course, was the man of the house, Horst. I couldn't imagine him in home-made shirts and pants: that just wouldn't cut it. Hymie became a treasured friend, supplying me for several years with wonderful fabrics. And he enjoyed delicious German breakfasts whenever he made the long trip from Manhattan.

One year Horst received a prestigious award from the NY Racing Association for one of his race track photos. The photo showed the legs of one of the thoroughbred horses in full stride, casting long shadows across the rippled soil of the track. The award was a great honor and was to be presented at the Belmont Ball, an annual fancy black-tie event.

Heavens, what to wear?

"Horst, we will be among New York's elite - the Who's Who in horse racing circles; the Whitneys, Vanderbilts, Phipps and other prominent families. I have never been near the rich and famous, never experienced this kind of fancy affair - I have nothing to wear." He said, "Make yourself a pretty dress from Hymie's beautiful fabrics."

I was excited, but also apprehensive and intimidated. How would I act in this totally foreign world of elegance and wealth? Would everyone look down at us? Would they even notice us? We could barely afford to rent a tuxedo for Horst.

But soon my excitement prevailed, the confidence in my abilities as a seamstress came back and I set out to find a suitable Vogue pattern for an evening dress. I chose a slim, full-length dress, sleeveless with a scoop neckline, simple but elegant. The fabric was a flowing, printed knit with abstract patterns of brown, black and white.

On the night of the ball, I felt confident and stylish in my home-made gown that had cost very little. I was grateful to my mother for passing her skills on to me and to Hymie for supplying the material. And, of course, to Horst for taking an award-winning photograph. I was so proud of him.

Everyone at the ball was very nice to us. They made us feel welcome among New York's upper crust. As far as I could tell, my home-made dress did not raise eyebrows. People included us and seemed to enjoy our story of coming to this country. They admired our way of speaking with an accent. What a confidence booster that night was for both of us. I needed it more than Horst, who already felt comfortable in any kind of situation. I learned that night that Americans in the upper classes are genuine people, down-to-earth people, not stuck up and snobbish. Back home in Germany, at least from what I remembered, the difference in social classes was much more pronounced. I don't believe we would have felt as comfortable there in a similar circumstance.

So, I say a heartfelt thank you to my friend, Hymie. He contributed an important chapter on our way to realizing the American Dream.

Horst and me at the Belmont Ball

Horst's award-winning photo

Horst enjoyed his job photographing activities around the training and grooming of the beautiful thoroughbred horses at Aqueduct and Belmont racetracks for the New York Racing Association. He left before sunrise most mornings and worked with his camera around the paddock and stables until early afternoon when he came home. Being around the world of the horse racing circuit allowed us to glimpse into the glamorous world of upper crust, high society New York - a world of money and prestige.

Sometimes Horst took us along to watch while he photographed the horses. I was hesitant about us being around those valuable horses. But Horst assured me it was alright for the girls and me to be there. And he was right. No one questioned our presence and the stable helpers were friendly. I felt so special and privileged to be admitted into this elite world.

It was magical to watch the early morning workouts. The horses exercising, with their trainers standing up high in their stirrups, guiding the groomed thoroughbreds around the paddock, trotting, galloping, their hooves throwing up dirt from the soft track, snorting with steam rising from their nostrils in the cool morning air. Back at the stables, stable hands rubbed the horses down. Sometimes we could touch one of those gorgeous animals.

And that's how on one of those early mornings we watched Secretariat (*yes, THE Secretariat*) working out in the paddock. Without understanding why, we could tell he was very special. Absolutely gorgeous and majestic with his dark brown coat glistening in the sun, his movements so very elegant and assured. We were permitted to touch and stroke him. Of course, we only had a vague idea of who he was and couldn't have known that he would become the most famous horse in history when he won the Triple Crown in 1973.

Horst's photo of Secretariat with his owner and trainer

When my brother Willi and later my parents visited, Horst arranged for them to spend time at the racetrack. I know they enjoyed this special treat.

Betting was a big part of the horse racing circuit and a constant temptation for people who worked there. I was glad that Horst never became a gambler; only once did he bet on a race. He won a nice amount and used his winnings to buy a gold bracelet for me, which I treasure to this day.

During the summer months the horse racing circuit moved to Saratoga Springs in upstate New York. Horst, of course, had to be there to document the activities with his camera. The girls and I came along and we spent fun times in the country. Horst rented a quaint cabin on nearby Garnet Lake for us so he could be close to the track. We had wonderful times up there, playing, hiking, swimming, reading, and cooking.

These race track visits are some of my favorite memories of those early years as immigrants.

Heidi, Birgit and me at the race track

The beauty of early mornings at the track

How did we merge two tightly packed cars into one?

The lean times of those first years were now behind us. While things were far from abundant, we felt very optimistic about making our way. The land of unlimited opportunities had given us our first taste of what that meant.

Horst had a passion for NSUs, an obscure small German car a little bigger than a VW Beetle. Convinced its engineering was the best of any car, he bought one of the first ones when they were available in the USA. That it broke down a lot didn't change his mind, he just learned to be an auto mechanic. Later he bought a second one, used, mostly for parts, so we always had one car that was in running condition.

One year, I think it was 1967 or 68, my youngest brother, Willi, visited us from Düsseldorf. It was wintertime and we made plans to spend Christmas in a cabin in the woods of Vermont. Both NSUs were running for once. We needed both cars to have enough room for the five of us and lots of baggage.

We left New York in a winter storm with frozen rain and sleet. Horst drove one NSU and I the other. We packed both cars to the brim with winter clothes and ski equipment for five people; skis, boots, poles, goggles, hats, parkas, etc. In addition, there were lots of wrapped Christmas gifts and Christmas decorations so we could have Christmas at our cabin.

The Big Squeeze

The trip should take about seven hours before arriving at our rented cabin in Chelsea, Vermont. As we made our way north, the sleet became worse and worse. The windshield wipers on Horst's car gave out. He had to roll down the window and wipe the windshield frequently with his left hand so he could see.

The roads were slick, making driving very slow and treacherous. When we got to Connecticut, Horst finally decided it was impossible to keep driving without working windshield wipers. Visibility was totally impaired. There was only one way forward: consolidate and keep going with the car that had working wiper blades. We exited the highway and found a gas station whose owner agreed to store the disabled car until we came back.

How did we fit two tightly packed cars into one? It was an almost impossible task, but we used ingenuity and determination to repack and move everything from one car into the other. We packed as much as possible on the roof rack and filled every nook and cranny inside. When we were ready to continue, the girls and Willi sat wedged together in the back seat. We filled all the spaces underneath our legs and on top of our laps with gear and packages. It was almost impossible to move. The trunk was overstuffed and hard to close. But we went back on the slick highway and continued our drive with many more hours ahead.

The sleet changed to snow, which made it easier to drive. We had lost several hours. It was the middle of the night and we were finally close to our destination. Suddenly, the car slipped through a turn and - *oh my!* - ended up on top of a tall snow drift. All was dark and quiet; no cars anywhere. Were we doomed to sleep in the car till morning? As luck would have it, we heard an approaching snowplow. We got the driver's attention, and he pulled our car off the drift - *what a relief!*

Soon we were turning into our cabin's snow-covered drive. We made it. Horst and Willi immediately started a fire in the cozy fireplace, which quickly warmed up the small cabin. Crawling under the covers never felt this wonderful.
The next day we woke up to an amazing winter wonderland; the cabin's roof and surrounding trees were thickly covered by newly fallen snow. The sun made everything sparkle; it was magical, and we were happy we didn't give up during the long and treacherous drive.

Horst and Willi walked through the deep snow around the cabin looking for a Christmas tree. The choices weren't great, but they agreed on a small tree and cut it down. It was really ugly with a crooked trunk and spindly branches but we set about decorating it with the ornaments we brought. It became the best loved Christmas tree we ever had.

For several months after returning home we still found small items stuck in the nooks and crannies of the NSU's trunk. A treacherous journey turned into a storybook Christmas for the five of us with cherished, life-long memories. The cabin in Vermont stayed a favorite destination for several years to come.

Being active girls, Birgit and Heidi had their share of mishaps, of course. One year in Vermont, Birgit, age 10, broke her leg skiing. It didn't stop her from getting around, though. She swung those crutches with gusto and determination to get to where she wanted to go. Another time her face got badly scratched up when, sledding down an icy ski slope, she slammed -face first- into a thorny bush. She had bloody gashes all over her face and had to be taken to the emergency room. Her swollen face was hard to look at, but in time it healed and thankfully left no lasting scars.

Another year at the cabin: shortly after the girls had gone to sleep in the bunk bed, we heard a huge *CRASH* coming from their bedroom - the top bunk bed with Heidi in it had collapsed onto the lower bunk where Birgit was sleeping. Luckily, after some scary moments of rescuing the two from the pile of wood and bedding, no one was hurt.

All that snow! Birgit and Heidi at work

The Problem With Y's And Z's

I'd loved being a stay-at-home mom for nine years, but with both girls in school, I became restless. I yearned to work again and to contribute to our family's financial wellbeing. I felt confident that I could pick up where I left off back home in Germany. My last job before leaving for America was as a secretary for a pharmaceutical publication. I was good at shorthand, typing, and organizational skills. When I had to leave that job to follow Horst to America, my boss gave me an excellent letter of recommendation.

In 1970, I said to Horst: *"It's time for me to get a job. I am ready to enter the workforce again. The girls are in school all day and you get home from the racetrack before they get home, so they'll be well taken care of. My English is good enough now. Just imagine - with a second income we could start saving for our future, a bigger apartment or even buying a house of our own."*

But how would I go about finding a job in this enormous city? Where should I start? The prospect felt overwhelming. I had learned to love the hustle and bustle of New York City, but finding someone who would hire me was intimidating and scary. But then I considered that thousands of immigrants before me had faced the same challenge and many succeeded. *Why not me too?*

I scanned the help wanted ads in The New York Times and made a few calls. It didn't take long until I had my first interview. All I remember - vividly - is that I badly flunked a shorthand and typing test. Why? Well, I made the nasty discovery that the German and English keyboards were not identical: the Y key and the Z key were transposed. Seems like a minor problem? It actually was a huge problem for me. When your trained hands fly across the keyboard, they automatically go to the familiar keys. Even one key out of order can mess you up completely.

To overcome this problem, I had to retrain my brain first and then my fingers. This was the time of manual typewriters and multiple carbon copies. Any typo had to be carefully erased with a special eraser, then typed over with the correct letter. It was also before copying machines. To make copies we inserted a sheet of black carbon paper between the original and the copies. Copy paper was a thin onion skin paper and came in different colors for specific uses. Mostly, we had to make two copies, one yellow for filing and a pink one for follow-up. You couldn't correct the copies so they revealed every typing error with dark smudges, no matter how perfectly you masked your mistake on the original. That was pretty embarrassing for a professional typist.

There was another problem: The German system of shorthand didn't work with the English language. Shorthand uses symbols for sounds and word combinations that are unique to each language and are ineffective in an unfamiliar language. When I tried it came out all wrong. How frustrating. I quickly realized how difficult it would be to enter the American workforce in my field of secretarial work.

It forced me to lower my expectations so I took an entry-level job as a collator. I worked in the dark, airless basement of a company, collating mountains of documents, eight hours a day, five days a week. That was my first job in America. Remember those aluminum collators? They were collapsible gadgets that could expand accordion style and had as many sections as needed. While collating, collating, collating, I let my mind wander. All the while, I was determined to prove my worth by becoming the world's best collator. There was a rhythm to it and I challenged myself to become faster and faster and faster. My boss really liked me and wanted to promote me. "*I want to be a secretary,*" I said with confidence.

But I could see in his eyes that would not be in my immediate future. Not with him, anyway. That's when my proven motto kicked in: *There's got to be another way.* Since I wanted to be a secretary again, how could I get the skills I needed? Should I learn the totally different English shorthand system? No, that would take too long and my English wasn't good enough yet. I did some research and discovered that there were textbooks in Germany for adapting the German shorthand method to the English language.

Yes, that's what I needed. I wrote an urgent letter to my sister in Düsseldorf: *"Friedel, I need your help. Please send me any books you can find on adapting German shorthand to the English language, as quickly as you can, danke, danke, danke."* The good sister she was, Friedel soon sent the textbooks I needed. I studied and practiced, practiced, practiced, with Horst dictating, first slower then faster and faster as I mastered the new system. It still was cumbersome and far from perfect, but I felt more confident.

What about the typing problem? My solution was to rent an American typewriter. I went to town typing for hours, hitting the keys over and over until I slowly got used to the new locations of the Y's and Z's. With determination, persistence and practice, it finally sank in. I told myself that what I had to go through was nothing compared to what professional immigrants had to endure. Physicians had to retake their exams and boards before they could practice in the States.

Soon I felt ready to offer my secretarial skills to employers. However, after a few interviews that went nowhere, I realized that my English just wasn't good enough yet. I became discouraged, but I was not willing to go back to being a collator - no, never!

One day a friend suggested *"Instead of applying for advertised jobs, place an ad in the paper yourself. Offer your skills and build yourself up a bit."* That sounded preposterous and aggressive. Who would want me? But the idea took hold and my confidence in myself returned. I knew I could be a good secretary, given the chance. So I took our friend's advice and called the New York Times. My ad read something like this: "Competent bilingual secretary, fluent in German and English, seeking employment." I had little hope. Would anyone even see the tiny ad?

The Phone Rings

But a miracle happened. The next day a nice lady called and asked me to come in for an interview. I dressed in my best business attire, looking sharp in my home-made gray gabardine suit (thanks, Hymie). On the subway into Manhattan, I pumped myself up mentally to look and sound confident and professional, although my heart was beating so fast it almost took my breath away. The office was on the 20th floor of 425 Park Avenue in downtown Manhattan, elegantly furnished with an atmosphere of quiet professionalism. I was in awe and felt very nervous. The lady who interviewed me was very kind. She put me at ease and treated me with respect.

My head was spinning. I wanted to make a good impression. It was all so overwhelming. Did I dare believe that I could get hired by this impressive firm? On my way home, I was quiet and exhausted. I didn't hold out hope. *"Horst, there's no way I'll hear from them, I am just not ready."* But the phone rang the next day and I had the job. I really had the job! I was so happy and giddy with delight. The company was Medchem, the German liaison office of famous drug maker Bayer AG - yes, the company that makes Bayer Aspirin. I couldn't believe my luck. I landed one of the best jobs - beyond my dreams and it paid even more than I hoped for. My boss was a nice man. He had just moved to New York from Germany and his English wasn't that great, so he didn't notice my lack of it either. In fact, he relied on me to correct his correspondence in English. I had to do a lot of bluffing to pull it off.

My real challenge, though, came from a colleague; a pleasant young lady who was the secretary to one of the other men. Our desks were right next to each other. She was a typing wizard. Her hands flew across the keyboard, and she rarely made a typo. How could I measure up to her? I was intimidated, but in no way did I want to let her see how poor my typing skills were compared to hers.

I hit the keys of my typewriter with outward confidence, trying to match her speed. This of course resulted in typo after typo, all the time pretending everything was fine. I discarded the messed-up pages and started over, giving the appearance that I was starting a new letter. This went on until - despite all the frantic dancing on the keys - I had produced some usable documents.

For every letter I finished, I probably had to toss four or five. While my colleague wasn't looking, I deposited the messed-up pages in my wastebasket. At the end of the day, my trashcan was full with discarded paper. Of course, I didn't want to raise suspicion by leaving this evidence of my inadequacy for the cleaning people to find.

I stuffed all that paper in my big purse and discarded it in a public trash can on my way home. My skills improved, and I totally loved working in that office. I felt on top of the world. It made me feel important to work with professional people who valued me. Looking down from the 20th floor onto Park Avenue with the jumble of honking, rushing yellow taxi cabs made me feel giddy with delight and awe. I had to pinch myself to believe I was really working in Manhattan. I had made a giant leap from the immigrant girl who didn't speak English.

I was lucky that no one ever discovered my deceit. I even got a glowing letter of recommendation when I left that job in 1974 to move to Denver.

I am 82 at this writing, happily retired after a fulfilling career and am enjoying time with family and friends. Travel, tennis and music still fill my days.

The girls grew into awesome, accomplished women with their own families. They gave me eight grandchildren and at last count, three great grandchildren. Horst moved back to Germany where he found the deserved recognition for his work. He is remarried to Christine and they stay in close touch with his family here. I found a new love in my golden years, Dr. Lowell Hansen.

I am truly blessed.

Lowell and me

Horst with grandkids in Colorado
(Chad is not in this picture)

167

THE GRANDKIDS' QUESTIONS

Foreword

I had an idea

My grandchildren should have a part

In my memoir

They were born long after

The stories in this book

It is for them I wrote about my early life

So they would learn how it was then...

I wanted them to have a voice

In my story

An opportunity to ask questions

I'm glad I did

I asked all eight of my grandchildren: "Think of five questions you would like to ask me about my life." All eight - Chad, Cliff, Heather, Carli, Shannon, Patricia, Trevor and Thomas - responded. Following is my attempt at answering forty questions. Similar and duplicate questions are grouped together.

Christmas Eve
Top from left: Heather, Trevor, Carli, Shannon, Omi Erika, Patricia, Thomas.
Bottom picture: Chad and Cliff

1. Questions About My Life In Germany

Shannon: What did Germany feel like when you lived in Düsseldorf?

I described in detail what life was like during the war in this memoir. So, to answer your question here, let me focus on what can be considered normal times after the war.

Ours was a working-class neighborhood with rows and rows of three-story apartment buildings. Few families owned their own homes in those times. For most of my childhood there were only a few cars in our neighborhood. People either walked, biked or used buses, streetcars or trains. In my early years we had no refrigerator, dishwasher, telephone or TV. Daily news came via radio and a daily newspaper.

Our mothers shopped every day for items they needed for that day's meals. People tended to gather outside the stores to exchange news about their families and gossip about their neighbors.

Without refrigeration it was tough to keep food cold during the warmer months, especially butter and milk. I was in my teens when we finally had a refrigerator ... such a welcome change.

Everyday life was much simpler then. Our parents were strict but gave us freedom and responsibility at a young age. We walked to and from school alone or with friends, we played outside unsupervised for long periods - even a whole day - and were sent on errands alone, many times having to take public transportation. We became independent and self-reliant early on. The older kids in our neighborhood took care of the younger ones by bringing them along on outings. Of course, our parents warned us not to talk to strangers and always stay together in groups. As is the case in any society, there were reports from time to time of bad people trying to harm children which made us extra careful and vigilant.

Our school day was shorter than here in America, we were home from school by lunchtime and had the afternoon for homework and play. Summer vacations were only four weeks long. We were graded on a scale from one to five with one being excellent, five unsatisfactory. All first graders looked forward to receiving their "Schultüte" (a tall, colorful, cone shaped cardboard container filled with treats and sweets) on their first day of school. Our school backpacks held books and a slate writing board with an attached sponge for erasing. Slate pencils were used to write on the boards.

Each summer we looked forward to the arrival of our local "Kirmes" (county fair). My favorite ride was the "Schiffschaukel" (boat swing). It allowed you to pump yourself higher and higher, eventually flipping all the way around, a full 360 degrees. This daring ride did not have any harnesses or safety features - which added to the thrill.

Carli: Did your mom make your clothes and did you stay close to your parents' siblings?

Yes, Mutti made most of the clothes for sister Friedel and me. Her sewing machine was rarely idle. She also made clothes for our dolls. I learned to sew from her, mostly by watching her. My first major purchase after coming to New York was a Singer sewing machine which is still in my basement today, mostly unused now. You can read more about my sewing activities in my story "Breakfasts with Hymie."

As far as staying close to my extended family in Germany - there were many aunts, uncles and cousins - we saw them often when we were kids, especially at family celebrations … birthdays, anniversaries, weddings, church confirmations, etc.

Most of my relatives lived in rural areas and we often visited them during summer vacations. We loved playing with our cousins in the countryside. I have fond memories of those times. On one of those visits, when I was ten, my cousin

Gerlinde taught me how to swim in a local pond. When I returned home I enrolled myself in a local swim club and swimming became a lifelong favorite sport for me.

You asked whether we remained close to our extended family. Over the years, as we siblings were busy with our own immediate families, our connections became less and less. That was especially true for me. Living so far away lessened my opportunities and desire to stay in touch. Often, I wonder about my cousins and how their lives turned out, but those are just meanderings of my mind. When I ask my siblings about this, their experiences are similar to mine.

Patricia and Trevor: What were your favorite traditions as a child and what is your happiest childhood memory? What new traditions did you form?

Christmas at home is by far my most cherished childhood memory. You probably noticed that I have a story in my memoir "Christmas at Home." I'm sure that while reading that chapter you recognized many elements I adopted for our Christmas celebrations here in Denver while you were growing up.

Easter was also a favorite of mine, not only when I was little, but especially when we siblings were older and would hide easter eggs for each other in impossibly difficult places. When someone needed help finding goodies, we spurred them on …"cold, warm, colder, really warm, hot, very hot!!!"

"Eier titschen" (egg cracking) always was part of our Easter fun (some of you kids adopted it). It works like this: Everyone takes a hard-boiled Easter egg and cracks one end against the end of another person's egg. Players take turns and the person whose egg remains intact at the end is the winner.

One beloved tradition that is not celebrated in the U.S. is St. Martin's Day. Each year on November 11, German children gather in remembrance of St. Martin who was a monk and patron saint of the poor. Legend tells of his charity on a snowy, wintry day long ago when Saint Martin offered half of his own cloak to a beggar who was shivering in the cold alongside a country road.

Children craft colorful paper lanterns with candles inside and walk in processions after dark in their neighborhoods. They carry their colorful and illuminated lanterns on long sticks, singing songs in honor of St. Martin. It is a beautiful sight to see the processions of brightly lit lanterns moving through the streets. At the end of the processions the children walk from house to house where they receive candy and baked treats, including Weckmänner (no translation necessary for you grandkids, right?).

St. Martin's Day holds fond memories for me. I loved making my own lantern, lighting the candle inside and walking with my friends through our neighborhood, anticipating being rewarded with tasty treats.

My own traditions started when I became a mom and grandmother (Omi). With the arrival of you kids I was ready and eager to start the traditions you all remember: Birthday sleepovers which included bike rides along Cherry Creek; bedtime stories; bubble baths with you disappearing under mountains of bubbles; waffle breakfasts with strawberries and whipped cream; taking your piggy banks - heavy with coins - to the Young Americans Bank, depositing half in your savings account and spending the rest at your favorite stores … the Wizard's Chest, Kazoo, Tattered Cover and the Gelato place. Oh, how I loved watching your excitement and delight. Often a little "subsidy" was needed from me when you were short on cash to buy a special treat you "had to have."

Not to forget the traditions I carried over from my childhood around Christmas: Baking Weckmänner (dough boys) decorated with raisins and almonds and "smoking" white clay pipes … then there were advent calendars with little surprises for each of the 24 days before Christmas. Together we built gingerbread houses, ending up with a sticky mess but delighted faces. One year six of you (Heather, Carli, Shannon,

Thomas, Patricia and Trevor) "invaded" my small kitchen, ready with bags of sticky icing and loads of candy, to compete with each other for the best gingerbread house. I remember it was a tie (even though one of the houses was precariously leaning to one side).

Best of all … our Christmas Eves together. It started in New York when Birgit and Heidi were little. They still believed that Christkindchen (Christ Child Angel) brought the presents. I don't remember when Santa Claus took over the privilege. The tradition continued when we moved to Denver and you grandchildren came along. In time our family was joined by boyfriends, husbands, girlfriends, wives, grandchildren and great grandchildren … until my small house was barely able to hold all of us. Throughout the years I carried forward my childhood traditions of real candles on the Christmas tree and family recipes for cookies and our special Christmas bread, Stollen. My heart is full with those happy memories.

Carli: What was the spark or feeling that made you know Opa was the right one?

I can't remember a particular spark; it was more of a gradual feeling. Opa was seven years older, he had a Highschool education while I only finished eighth grade. He spoke English and I admired him for his knowledge and "sophistication." I loved listening to him for what seemed like hours. He made topics like science, biology and geography fascinating for me. I also admired him for having traveled solo to France and England and I loved to hear his stories about his adventures camping, meeting people and seeing places I could only dream about. He taught me how to dance. We practiced without music in his parents' apartment. I was impressed with his photography … his talent to capture everyday life in a pure and captivating way.

And he was handsome with a great smile. He was my first steady boyfriend and I was smitten. Carli, I assume you were thinking about you and Zack when you asked this question?

Thomas: What did you do when you had Birgit at such a young age and how did you make that work?

As the saying goes, "Life is what happens to you while you are busy making other plans."

Being pregnant at age 18 was not what Horst and I planned. It changed the trajectory of both our lives. We were forced to adjust our plans for the future. I felt I had disappointed my family and felt the stigma of those times.

Opa and I made the best of it. We married and focused on the important job of becoming parents.

Our families helped us deal with the situation. It was almost impossible for us to find our own place to live because reconstruction after the war had not yet caught up with the tremendous need for housing. When your mom was born, Opa's parents, Max and Alma, opened their small apartment to us and we lived with them in cramped quarters until Opa left for Canada. While Opa was away, his mother took care of Birgit during the week while I worked.

To be sure, ours was a rough beginning and difficult at times, but we got through it all by taking responsibility and charging ahead with a good attitude and optimism. Baby Birgit was loved by her family and grew up and thrived.

This tough situation taught us many lessons and helped us become independent and self-sufficient. We will always be grateful for the loving help from our families.

2. Questions About The War

There are several questions about my experiences during WWII. I will keep my answers here short and refer you to the child of war story where I write extensively about the war.

Chad: What was it like living in an environment where your home was destroyed by bombs? Luckily, it's so far removed from anything we grandkids have experienced.

Thomas: What was going on in your head during the war? Were you too young to understand or were you as afraid as everyone else?

For me as a small child the things I experienced felt normal. I had no memories of an intact world. The rubble around me was a playground. It didn't matter that I had few things to wear or play with … I had no way to compare it to anything different. My family was around me, what else did I need? Only when I was older did the enormity of what happened sink in. By that time our lives had returned close to normal with reconstruction in full swing.

It was different for my two older brothers, Erhard (8 years older) and Horst (4 years older). Their stories include recollections of fear and dread.

Carli: What was it like to be so close to the bombs and to see your home bombed?

I was too young to feel much fear or maybe I was afraid but don't remember it. I remember seeing a dead person - covered up - lying in the street, but I don't remember being frightened by it. I saw unexploded bombs lying around and sensed fear in the people around me, but I don't remember being afraid myself - except for the time when I was lost in the mass of people heading to the bomb shelter. I remember seeing our destroyed home and seeing the despair in my family's faces.

Carli: How was the food during the war? Did you have food rationing?

Food shortages caused great hardship. Supply chains were devastated and the little food that was available was strictly rationed. I clearly remember being hungry much of the time. Scrounging for food for our family was a never-ending job for our parents until help came from other countries, especially America. Most of the people in the bombed-out cities became malnourished.

Nothing that could be eaten was wasted; potato and vegetable peels were cooked, bones were ground and mixed with flour and water into a kind of dumpling, soups were made with water, flour and seasonings. Fish, beef, chicken heads, tails and bones were cooked; *nothing* was thrown away.

Memories of that time have stayed with me throughout my life, they instilled in me an appreciation and gratitude for our abundance of food.

Carli: How did you escape the Russian occupation?

Our escape from east to west Germany takes up an important part of this memoir, a most dramatic story about risking our lives to cross a dangerous border to get back home. I remember experiencing fear during our escape, I believe it was mostly due to sensing the fear in my parents. I remember feeling tired, so very tired. It is truly a miracle we made it across alive and our family was eventually reunited. If my parents hadn't taken that big risk, we would have been stuck in East Germany under Communist rule for many years, cut off from our families in the West ... maybe even until German reunification in 1990.

Thomas: If the war never happened would you still live in Germany?

Possibly, although I had great curiosity in my teen years and wanted to experience other places. I dreamt of working in countries like England or France temporarily (or a year or two). I was fascinated with America but that seemed too big of a dream (or was it?). I guess that in normal times I might have had the opportunity for higher education and a promising career path in Germany which could have led to a happy life in my home country. But we will never know. I feel content with the way my life turned out.

3. Questions About Going To America

Heather: When you first came to New York what aspects of living in America were surprising and unexpected for you?

Practically everything was surprising: the enormity of the city, the dizzying architecture of the skyscrapers, the vast subway system with several stories of underground tunnels and the sheer masses of people going about their daily lives. It all seemed so chaotic. Yet it all worked, like a humongous beehive, millions of comings and goings day and night that all worked out somehow. This became a constant fascination for me and it made me feel glad I could be part of it.

It was surprising and delightful how friendly and inclusive Americans were. We were welcomed with friendly curiosity. New York was and still is a melting pot of many nationalities. We never felt discriminated against. Yet, one thing that was unexpected and astonished me was that racial segregation still existed. The public bathrooms at Jones Beach were labeled "black" and "white." This seemed unbelievable to me. Back home in Germany, the few black people we came across were treated like everyone else.

Trevor: What were the differences between your childhood in Germany and your children's childhoods in America?

This is a complex question, Trevor, and not easily answered in a few sentences because it involves several societal and cultural aspects and time periods: the circumstances in Germany during and after the war, blending German and American cultural factors after our move to New York and what I learned from observing American ways of raising children.

During and after the war, we kids had to become independent early on. We mostly played by ourselves with little to no supervision as long as we came home for dinner before dark. We had few toys but used our imaginations to invent games and fun activities.

We were taught the importance of discipline and obeying rules, above all - honoring our parents. We learned that bad behavior had consequences of punishment which shaped us into responsible adults. A stern look put us in our place; no back talking, no whining.

Looking back, I feel that some of the strict disciplines were a bit cruel, i.e., "children should be seen, not heard." It wasn't the best environment to foster self-confidence.

In contrast - without generalizing too much - American children often seem less disciplined and are easily forgiven for misbehavior. I sometimes feel that today's children are being coddled and overly protected. On the positive side, American children receive a great deal of attention and praise which helps them develop a higher self-esteem.

With our girls, Birgit and Heidi, we combined a little bit of both worlds. We taught them more by example rather than strict rules. They learned to be self-expressive and confident by emulating their American friends and families. I would say it was a successful commingling of cultures.

Chad: What do you miss about living in the US vs. Germany?

It's now over sixty years since we arrived in America. Much has changed since then. Back then we didn't have the choice, variety and quality in goods we have now, from bread to beer to coffee and beyond.

In those early years in the US, we would often discuss the things we missed with our immigrant friends. We lamented a lack of quality and style in many of the consumer goods, i.e., polyester clothing vs. wool or cotton, real vs. synthetic leather, fine cotton vs. wash-and-wear.

Worst of all (luckily this trend didn't last long): plastic slipcovers for upholstered furniture. Even today, older Americans cringe when they remember sitting on the hard, slick plastic slipcovers … causing them to slide off the sofa or chair. It was especially bad in the summer heat when bare legs and arms got stuck on the plastic.

We also had a hard time adjusting to the throw away culture here - discarding things before they were worn out … I still mended our socks.

Americans drank little wine when we first arrived, they preferred whisky and mixed drinks, which we liked and often drank, especially Whiskey Sours. We missed freshly baked breakfast rolls and hearty breads, crusty and wholesome. We shook our heads at Wonder Bread. To this day I have never bought a loaf. Coffee tasted more like flavored water to us compared with the robust but smooth coffee at home. And coffee served in thick mugs? At home we drank coffee from delicate china cups with saucers. American beer tasted watered down to us compared with the rich and tasty local beers at home.

Something else we missed: quiet evenings and weekends. Back then in Germany, most shops closed around 7 p.m. during the week and - with certain exceptions - were totally closed on Saturdays and Sundays. Evenings and weekends were spent with family and friends. There was an atmosphere of calm and togetherness - afternoon coffee and cake (Kaffee Klatsch) - and walks in the park. This contrasted starkly with the constant busyness in our new country: 24/7 shopping, 24-hour groceries, going to the mall for entertainment.

Much of that has changed over the years as a result of international travel. Germans visiting the US adopted many things and ideas they liked, and vice versa: Americans traveling in Europe imported many customs and products they enjoyed while abroad. Today the differences are still there, but much reduced. We now have a great selection of artisan breads, first rate coffee, quality wines and craft beers. We can choose from an incredible variety of imported goods. Hershey's chocolate has been surpassed by many European fine chocolates, my favorite being Lindt.

I still miss riding the trains, especially the fast ICE (Intercity Express). I love the sensation of sitting comfortably in my seat, watching the countryside fly by outside my window as the train seemingly floats at high speed on the gleaming tracks. I miss being able to walk along the Rhein promenade, watching the barges floating by in either direction - laboring hard moving upstream towards the river's beginning in Switzerland or swiftly sailing downstream to where it empties into the Atlantic Ocean in Holland.

I will always miss the lovely church bells and look forward to their sound on my trips home. Some of them still announce the time of day: One gong for the quarter hour, two for the half hour, three for three-fourth and four for the full hour followed by one gong each for what hour of day it is … up to twelve gongs for noon and midnight. Chad, when you visited Germany, do you remember hearing the church bells?

I also still yearn for familiar foods: Morning Brötchen (rolls) fresh from the oven, roasted goose (your great grandma Elfriede made the world's best by far), mouthwatering tortes and pastries (especially those made by my brother Horst, the pastry chef). On my visits home I always enjoy a meal of matjes herring (herring filets cured in salt) with onions, dill and sour cream over fried golden potatoes. I miss the tasty local beers served in small thin glasses. Of course, I miss seeing family and friends.

Cliff: Have you ever wished you had remained in Germany or moved back one day?

Did I regret coming here and wanted to move back? No. While I will always love my home country Germany, I never had a serious wish to return. This country has been very good to me. I was given many opportunities to grow and thrive here. I feel well-grounded and grateful for our growing family. It is important for me, though, to visit my German family often and keep in touch regularly. Those trips home are always filled with happy gatherings of the ever growing family. I am especially glad that I was able to take you kids to meet your German family. Those trips were a special joy. I was so proud to introduce my wonderful grandchildren to my siblings and their families.

I am thankful for the close and loving long distance connections I have with my siblings and their families. Many of them have visited us over the years in New York and Denver. Those were always joyous and fun filled times.

Patricia: What was New York culture like when you moved there? Were there tight knit immigrant groups? How did it compare to the home you left behind?

New York is a melting pot of thousands of ethnicities and cultures. New immigrants like us were welcomed. Starting a new life in another country has great challenges and many new immigrants formed support groups with their countrymen. New York is home to many of those ethnic neighborhoods ... Little Italy, Germantown, Chinatown, Irish Americans, to name just a few. We could have joined a German group, but preferred to assimilate by spending time with and learning from the people in our new neighborhoods. We enjoyed the welcoming ways of most Americans and wanted to fit in. We also formed our own immigrant group with several young immigrant families from Germany, Finland and Switzerland which helped us stay connected to our home country.

Our open attitude to new things allowed us to chart our own course in a country that respected and fostered personal ambition. I never felt discrimination or ridicule because of my poor English. We were not discouraged from pursuing the American Dream. The opportunities were there and it was up to us to work hard in our pursuits. The people we met accepted us and welcomed us as friends and neighbors.

That said, there were things we didn't like … the constant noise, dirty sidewalks, being packed like sardines in subway cars during rush hour, the oppressive heat and humidity in summer … but that was just part of the incredible diversity of life in an enormous city of eight million people.

By now, Patricia, I'm sure you can tell I loved New York … and I still do. Would I want to live there again? No, life in Denver has been wonderful for me and our growing family. I still love to visit and enjoy watching movies that are filmed in New York … recognizing many places from living there. I relish the memories.

Trevor: What were the best and the worst parts of coming to America?

The best part was the promise of starting a new life in an exciting new place. We loved taking it all in with curiosity and open minds. Everything was new and different, from going shopping to sightseeing. From toothpaste to laundry soap, everything had a different name and unfamiliar look. I had never seen or tasted artichokes or avocados.

The architecture and buildings looked so different from the ones at home. Everything was bigger than at home … huge and impressive. We walked around Manhattan with our faces tilted up until our necks started hurting. Masses of people and cars everywhere, pulsing with life, people from all over the world speaking in many different languages. And the immensity of the subway system, several stories deep underneath the streets, its screeching and rumbling noises could be heard through the steel grates in the sidewalks.

Often we encountered curiosities like the one time we saw a woman casually walking her donkey in Central Park. Only in New York!

The worst part was that we missed our families and had no idea when we would see them again. There was a constant stream of letters to and from home. Phone calls were prohibitively expensive, we could only afford to call our loved ones during holidays and no more than three minutes per call. During those calls we couldn't really understand much because we were all talking at the same time. When your mom was born in 1963, Opa announced her birth via Western Union telegram rather than spending money on a phone call. One Christmas we sent home the recorded voices of Birgit and Heidi. I was told there were tears when the recordings were played while the family was together. They missed us and we missed them.

Patricia: Which was scarier, being alone in Germany while Opa was in Canada or coming to America alone?

Definitely being alone with little Birgit in Düsseldorf. Canada seemed so very far away. While I was hopeful for us to be reunited, occasionally dark thoughts kept me wondering "will I ever see him again?" "What if he is lost in the vastness of the Canadian wilderness?" "Will he change his mind about wanting to be with Birgit and me?" The year we were apart seemed really long. But then his letter arrived: "Erika, it's time for you to come join me in New York."

Making the journey alone with Birgit to New York was not scary at all … we were going to be together again, embarking on a better life.

Shannon: What was life like with Opa?

Life with Opa was never boring. His creative spirit made him do things "outside the box." We were constantly on the go to places he wanted to discover. Being short of money didn't stop him from exploring New York and several of the eastern states. When we went skiing - to save money - we bought one lift ticket and switched jackets after lunch. That way, one of us stayed with the girls while the other one skied. Other times we put our skis on our backs and hiked up a hill to ski down rather than pay for a ticket. One year, Opa found this cheap, extremely remote cabin in Vermont where we spent memorable vacations, one of which is the subject of the story "Vermont" in this book.

Opa was never without his camera bag. As a freelance photographer he documented everything we did plus he was always on the lookout for a feature story that he could sell to newspapers and magazines. Like most couples, we did have our differences but he and I agreed on most things and rarely argued. Opa was very supportive and never stood in my way when I wanted to do something by or for myself.

In his work as press photographer, Opa received press passes to many events that we would not ordinarily have had access to. One time he did a photo story on a very famous opera star, Theresa Stratas. He interviewed and photographed her in her dressing room at the famed Metropolitan Opera in New York. Sometimes he took us along to interesting places like art galleries, concerts and sporting events, all free of charge for us because he had a press pass.

When Opa wasn't working on his photography, we could often find him working on his NSU, an obscure German car brand. It constantly broke down, so he bought another used NSU just for the parts.

One thing about Opa we now chuckle about but drove me crazy at the time - he seriously believed that traffic rules did not apply to him. He argued that he was such a good driver and should not have to obey those "silly" rules. Many speeding tickets and other traffic violations did not change his mind. Anyone else in the family that stubborn?

4. Questions About Life Issues

Patricia: Who was your role model when you grew up and how did it shape your life?

My mother set a wonderful example for how to live a loving and caring life. Even after she was gone and whenever I was uncertain about something I would ask myself, *"what would Mutti do?"*

I also greatly admired my oldest brother Erhard for his drive and accomplishments. He excelled in everything he did. It was always important to me (and still is) to make him proud of me.

Over the course of my life there were, of course, many other people I admired who I tried to learn from and emulate. Bill Daniels was one of those people. He was my mentor and my friend. He saw so much more in me than I dared see in myself and encouraged me to grow beyond my most ambitious dreams and to give 110% to any effort. I learned from him to strive for win-win situations in business dealings and in personal life. He'd say "always give a little more and take a little less."

Cliff: What is the "truest" thing you have encountered, learned, or discovered in your life?

This philosophical question has been tackled by great thinkers since time began. Maybe the "truest" thing will never be known? Or is it so obvious that we overlook it?

I have an advantage by having lived so long, over eighty years of observation and personal experience. They say "wisdom comes with age," so let me try…

Looking back and reflecting on my life and the lives of those around me, I know one thing: a loving heart can overcome many difficulties and bring happiness to ourselves and those we love. Can it be that simple? I believe that choosing love can smooth out life's wrinkles. When we give love… unconditionally… it comes back to us many times over.

I confess that, like many of us, I haven't always been able or willing to let love be my guide. We humans are inherently flawed; there are so many things that interfere… and I have known and been challenged by them all: insecurity, envy, distrust, doubt; being judgmental, jealous, impulsive, fearful, selfish… and I can go on. Those who make LOVE their "truest" thing are to be envied and admired.

There is another "true" thing I believe in: gratitude. No matter how bad things are, there is always something we can be grateful for. I love a mantra that has been a steady guide for me: "Expect good things with confidence and accept them with gratitude." Often we get impatient and expect immediate results. It pays to allow for positive thinking and time to solve many of our problems.

Heather: If you had to pick, what would be your happiest memory?

How can I choose just one? There are so many happy memories. But here's one from my early years in this country that often pops into my mind.

It's New York, the summer of 1969. Since arriving in New York in 1961 we have settled down nicely. We live in a two-bedroom apartment in Flushing, Queens. Opa has a very good job with the New York Racing Association. We have made friends with three other immigrant families and have become inseparable. We are each other's "ersatz" (substitute) families. Together we have five children close in age and they are like cousins.

I am about 30 years old at the time, Birgit is eleven and Heidi is six years old. On this particular day our little immigrant group drives north to one of our favorite parks, "Pound Ridge", about an hour's drive north of New York City. The children are busy playing with their Barbie dolls among the trees, building make-believe villages and acting out scenes of ordinary life. We adults are relaxing in the sun with a good book or simply enjoying the beautiful surroundings. Our picnic table is filled with a variety of homemade foods and drinks.

As I take in this happy scene, my heart fills with a deeply felt joy and gratitude. I think to myself "we made it… this is the happiest time of my life."

Chad: As a young woman, what were some of your dreams for your future?

Thomas: Is there an event/moment in your life where you wish you had done something different?

I believe what is important is that I accepted the consequences of my choices and made the best of them. Looking back now of course I ask myself if my choices were good or not. I wonder if I should have taken a different path and what my life would have been like. And, yes, I can think of many things I could have done differently.

Overall, I chose what felt right at the moment and fit the circumstances. And those choices made me who I am today... a content, grateful and accomplished woman.

From an early age I fantasized about leaving my hometown to experience other places. My imagination painted a bigger world outside of the only place I knew - Düsseldorf. I thought a lot about going to England as an au pair (nanny), which was very popular among young women at that time.

Closer to home, I would have loved to design window displays for large retail stores. Often, I stood in front of the beautiful window displays admiring every detail. They were especially gorgeous around Christmas time. I dreamt of helping to create these mini worlds. But I had to be more realistic and practical. I was expected to contribute to the household right out of school. At age 14, after finishing 8th grade, I began a three-year apprenticeship in an office with the goal of becoming a secretary. Half of what I earned went towards the family's household expenses.

Our character is shaped by the kaleidoscope of how we handle our good and not so good choices. That's how we learn and grow. Some of the best lessons in life we learn from the mistakes we make. What we consider failures or shortcomings can teach us valuable lessons; they help us grow. In my case, I used those experiences to find creative solutions, using my best skills and talents combined with a positive and forward-looking attitude.

Shannon: What have you found joy in over your life?

Shannon: What is the most important part of your life?

My greatest joy and most important part of my life is being a mother and grandmother. I would never have guessed that I would have eight grandchildren. And I heard the first cry of each of you, how amazing is that? For most of you, it happened while I was waiting outside the delivery room. As the nurses were going in and out of the room, I tried to get information: "How is it going?" "Everything OK?" When I knew it was imminent, I pressed my ear to the door until the unmistakable sound was heard — my grandchild's first cry. Eight grandchildren and eight first cries — each strong but already individual at the time of your birth.

I experience joy listening to my favorite classical music. I can't imagine my life without it. It is food for my soul. It has been a joy for me to introduce you, Shannon, to the world of opera. I liked taking you to some of the live streamed performances of the New York Metropolitan Opera. You loved being the youngest person by far in the audience of mostly older opera fans. Watching your rapt attention and joy made me happy and proud. Maybe that little seed will grow and you will tell your children about the time you learned about opera.

Perhaps the best kind of happiness is finding joy in small everyday things… my first cup of coffee in the morning, watching the birds and squirrels in my backyard, being with people I love, learning new things, watching the waves crash to shore at The Sea Ranch, taking walks on a crisp spring day under blue skies, seeing the first hummingbirds at my feeder after a long winter, discovering birds nesting in my birdhouse.

Then there is the joy I feel when I look back at my life and know it was good.

Heather: What advice would you give a younger version of yourself?

I would say "Erika, enjoy the journey of living and trust that the bumps in the road get smoothed out in time. Always maintain a positive attitude, look for the good in any situation. Don't forget to see humor in life's roller coaster and stay humble – give more and take less.

Also, "Don't give up on your dreams and don't pressure yourself into thinking you have to do it all at once. It is never too late to pursue something you are passionate about, even later in life." Case in point, I was able to realize two early dreams much later in my life. First, from an early age I loved learning new things and longed for a more formal education. At age 45, I went back to school and earned my MBA.

Second, my love for playing the piano came true when I bought one at age 75 and began taking lessons. Who knows... maybe some of my other dreams will still come true?

Looking back, there is one thing that served me well in times of seemingly insurmountable difficulties: I would tell myself *"there's got to be another way."*

I would also tell my younger self, "believe in yourself and always be true to who you are." I say this because there was a time during my career in Denver when I felt I wasn't good enough. I compared myself to my colleagues and found many things lacking. I expended a lot of energy trying to emulate the people around me. I told myself the lie that if only I could be like them, I would surely be better at my job and be more respected. *"Well, my dear younger me, that did not work."* The pretending made me feel self-conscious, isolated and miserable. My self-esteem took a turn for the worse.

When I finally decided to accept fully who I am, I started acting in natural, open and genuine ways. I embraced and realized that being ME was enough. I recognized later how foolish it was to try to be someone else. Dear Me: *"You are*

194

enough just as you are. Be open and empathetic, share your feelings and people will respect and embrace you."

Chad, Cliff and Shannon: How did the difficulties in your early years benefit you during the course of your life?

Living through the war and its aftermath and witnessing the struggles of my family and the greater community created a deep-seated respect for the enormous capacity of people to endure, overcome and eventually thrive. It gave me the confidence that no matter what life throws my way, I am able to handle it. Roadblocks are opportunities to find solutions. I gained an instinctive can-do attitude that allowed me to accept difficulties with an eye toward finding the positive in any situation and using creative ways to make things better.

Upon further reflection about my early confrontations with catastrophic events, I theorize that maybe as a five-year old I subconsciously protected myself by going into denial when frightening things happened around me, blocking out of my mind what I couldn't comprehend.

And maybe that denial mode stayed with me throughout my life as a protection when faced with setbacks and difficulties.

Trevor: How have you seen God in your life?

I was raised in the Lutheran faith by my family, was christened as a baby and confirmed at age fourteen. Opa and I were married by Pastor Halfmann whom I loved and admired. Both Birgit and Heidi were christened and confirmed in the Lutheran church. I didn't question my Christian beliefs until in my thirties when doubts and skepticism caused me to stray. I explored modern spiritual ideas for several years, but never totally lost my faith and returned to it later in my life. I still have many questions and doubts, but in my heart, I feel the presence of God.

A note about religion in the Germany of my youth: The two major religions were Catholic and Protestant (Lutheran). A big divide existed between the believers of both faiths. "Mixed marriage" meant one spouse was Catholic, the other Protestant. This was frowned upon and created severe discourse in families. Two of my siblings, Horst and Friedel, married Catholic partners which caused a rift in our family. There was a shouting match between my father and his brother Kurt who said: "How can you allow this?" It didn't stop the couples' determination but left a bitter taste in the family. As time went by, this discrimination was tempered and later disappeared.

Every day I feel blessed and give thanks to God for the abundance in my life, especially for my family and friends. I turn to God in times of need. Praying gives me comfort and hope. I feel God's love and care.

Trevor: What's a risk you have taken that you never regretted?

I have to say that leaving my family to follow Opa to America was a really big risk. We had very little money and a small child, Birgit, who was 1-½ years old when Opa left Germany. Where would we live? How would we afford to buy household necessities in an unfamiliar place? Will Opa find work? Will I be able to work with the few words of English I knew? Will we get homesick?

Fortunately, it all worked out and I never regretted making that big move.

Heather: I admire you for maintaining so many friendships over the years. How have those friendships influenced you?

Reflecting on what makes a good friendship, I ask: how do friends enter our lives? What makes some friends stay in our lives for a short time while others stay close to us for a lifetime? How can we nurture important relationships? Can one have too many or too few friends? Why do some long-distance friendships thrive? What do friendships add to our lives? How do friendships change over time? Do friends pick us or do we seek them out?

I confess, Heather, I don't have good explanations about these mysteries but I have some ideas how friendships work based on my own experiences.

Friendships are gifts. They come to us without being coerced, they blossom when we embrace them with openness, honesty and trust. The more we give of ourselves to a friend, the more we get in return.

Not all friendships last. Sometimes we grow apart in the normal course of life, ending some friendships and starting new ones. The best friendships are those where there are no demands made, we accept each other for who we are, we support each other and enjoy being in each other's lives. Good friendships survive after stretches of little or no contact.

When the phone rings after a long pause it is as though we were never apart: "How have you been, great to catch up with you."

I am grateful for the friends who are a part of my life and who share their lives with me. We learn from each other and enhance each other's lives in immeasurable ways.

Patricia: What was your most "enjoyable" struggle, something that was really hard at the time, but resulted in an "oh so sweet" reward?

There is no question in my mind that going back to school at age 43 to get my MBA was a huge struggle and effort. There were times when I had doubts if I could make it. Falling asleep over my textbooks at 2 a.m. and then leaving for work five hours later was no picnic. But how sweet it was to wear my cap and gown on graduation day and receive my diploma: "Erika Luise Schafer - Master of Business Administration."

Thomas: How is it that you are such an amazing and wonderful human being?

Oh Thomas, thank you for that accolade, you are very generous. Really, I don't see myself as being that special. I guess having had to overcome challenges in my early life strengthened me. Also, I think I was born with a positive disposition. It helped me to find something good in any situation - 'what can I do to make things better?' 'How can I contribute to the happiness of the loved ones in my life?'

Anyone who acts out of compassion and empathy for others, works hard and remains humble and grateful is indeed a wonderful human being.

5. Questions About Moving To Colorado

Cliff: What spurred your move to Colorado and how did it feel in contrast to moving to New York?

After living in New York for about ten years, we became restless and disenchanted with the city. We decided that in the long run, New York was not a good place to raise our daughters. More and more we were bothered by the high cost of living, the incessant noise, the masses of people everywhere, the packed subways, increasing crime and stifling heat in summer. We started to consider places with a better quality of life where we would have a chance to get ahead.

Adding to that was a scary incident when a creepy stranger closely followed your mom from school all the way home. Frightened, she started running until she reached our apartment. This experience haunts her still after so many years.

In the early 70s, our friends Helena and Peter with their son Jan moved to Denver and kept reporting how great it was. We visited them one year and soon thereafter decided to make the move. We were impressed with the endless blue skies, the majestic Rocky Mountains and the fabulous snow conditions.

Compared to skiing back east, it was pure heaven to ski on Colorado's champagne powder. Two years after that visit we made the move. Both Opa and I quit our jobs in New York and ordered a moving van.

Birgit was fifteen and Heidi ten. We arrived in Denver in March of 1974. As before in New York, Opa had gone ahead to find a place for us to live. Housing was so much less expensive than in New York and we had saved enough money to afford a down payment. Together with our friend Helena, Opa decided on the house at 4675 South Lewiston Way in Aurora. We bought it for $30,000. I did not see the house until we moved in. Luckily, I approved and was happy that now we were homeowners.

Adjusting to life in Colorado was not easy. The girls missed their friends and I missed New York. There were times in the beginning when I felt we had made a terrible mistake. But slowly, with the help of our friends, Helena and Peter, I learned to appreciate life here. The girls adjusted to their new schools and made new friends. We started to enjoy the many wonderful things Colorado has to offer. Life was simpler than in New York, people were friendly and helpful. We enjoyed the endless blue skies and magnificent sunsets. We loved hiking in the grandeur of the Rocky Mountains.

The contrast between moving to New York and then Denver was huge. Moving to New York was enormously exciting combined with the opportunity of starting a new life after the struggles at home. The move to Denver was a big culture shock compared to New York. In the beginning it felt to me like moving backwards. After I got the secretarial job at Daniels & Associates, which was exciting and stimulating, it helped me adjust to the move and even feel glad about it.

And look at us now: our family grew by leaps and bounds. Soon there were boyfriends, engagements, weddings and eight grandchildren, three great grandchildren and counting. At last count there were twenty of us. I feel truly blessed that most of our family is close by and thriving… we made a good decision to raise our family in this beautiful place.

Heather: What prompted you to get your masters degree at the University of Denver and was it difficult returning to school after being a Mom? Why did you get into Real Estate?

This question is complex and requires a somewhat lengthy answer. After we moved from New York to Denver in 1974, I started working as a secretary at cable TV company Daniels & Associates. I was promoted several times. In order to live up to the increasing responsibilities, I felt I needed to have an MBA degree - Master of Business Administration. I discovered that the University of Denver offered an Executive MBA program geared toward business people who wanted to pursue a degree while working at the same time.

When I found out that I needed an undergraduate degree to qualify for the program but all I had in the way of credentials was a GED (General Education Degree), my lifelong mantra *"there's got to be another way,"* kicked in. I discussed my situation with the head of the program, Ron Gist, and made a deal with him. He said "If you successfully complete an undergraduate math class and if you pass the GMAT (Graduate Management Admissions Test), I'll make an exception and admit you."

I enrolled in a basic math class where I shared the classroom with people in their twenties - I was 43. I hadn't been in a classroom since my teens and… yes... I felt pretty out of place. I got some skeptical looks, but I managed to get an A in the class. Your mom, Heidi, who was also a student at DU at the time, coached me for the GMAT exam which I barely passed. My boss, Bill Daniels, wrote a wonderful letter of recommendation. *I WAS IN!*

Because of my limited formal education, I soon realized what a tough road it was for me. For the next two years I worked full time and studied evenings and weekends.

200

There was no time for friends and little time for family. But I was energized and worked very hard, graduating in the top third of my class in August 1985 at age 45.

Did it help me with my job? That is hard to quantify, but it definitely raised my self-esteem. I felt I could speak the same language as my colleagues. It's one of the hardest yet best things I ever did for myself.

Why did I get into Real Estate? From an early age I always had a love for architecture and design, but I never had an opportunity to pursue them as a career. While at Daniels I was given the responsibility to oversee the design and construction of the company's new headquarters building in Cherry Creek North. I worked with architects, interior designers and contractors to build this beautiful building. It allowed me to realize my passions in an unexpected way.

Thus, when I was laid off from my job after a company merger in 1989, it was natural for me to focus on opportunities in real estate development. Bill Daniels liked my ideas and offered to become my financial partner in a new business: E. Schafer Associates, Inc. I got my real estate brokers license and looked for opportunities to buy and develop properties in the Cherry Creek area. Our first project involved building a four-unit townhouse project, and another four-unit project followed. Then a third project - seven high end townhomes, all in Cherry Creek North - was completed in 1996.

Being a woman developer in an almost exclusively male business was very hard. There were lots of sleepless nights, but in the end, it worked out. My last project, the seven units on Clayton Street, now has a reputation for being among the best in Cherry Creek North. Because of my inexperience and some tough market conditions at that time I didn't get rich, but I feel proud whenever I walk by there.

The outgrowth of that venture was a career as a real estate broker specializing in high-end homes which ended up much more lucrative than being a developer.

Chad: Why did Opa and you divorce?

Our story is different from most. As you know, Opa and I are still close to this day. He simply couldn't make it here in Denver. His type of photography wasn't in demand and it was a great struggle for him to make a living in his field. Disillusioned, in 1978 he started to talk about the possibility of going back to Germany. Denver had been a professional disappointment for him and the thought of moving back home gave him renewed energy and optimism. And so, for the third time in his life he made a big move and started from scratch. How he managed to jump start a new career at age 46 is an amazing and inspiring story - one he should tell you personally sometime.

So, you see, after living apart for a while, on two different continents, Opa and I needed to be free to live our individual lives. We decided it was best for both of us to end our marriage. When we met with our attorney, Patricia Stone, to divide our assets and sign the papers, she looked at us and said: "I have handled hundreds of divorces; you two must be the most reasonable couple I ever dealt with."

Opa's return to Germany brought him the success he had yearned for. He became one of the most respected photographers in Germany with numerous exhibitions and media recognitions. Often, he is compared to the renowned photographer Alfred Stieglitz. Opa published more than fifteen books of his works. He is happy living in his birth country, but misses the family he left behind in Denver. He and his second wife Christine visit us as often as they can and enjoy spending time with all of us.

Even now after so many years we keep in touch and fondly remember our times together and raising two beautiful and accomplished daughters, Birgit and Heidi.

Cliff: We grandkids have enjoyed and learned from the tradition of our birthday piggy banks. The concept of saving - little things adding up. Where did the idea come from?

In my youth money was always tight in my family. Observing the struggles made a deep impression on me and I developed a strong desire not to be without money. I became a lifelong saver. Even during lean times, I tucked away whatever I could.

Your piggy banks were a way for me to teach you about the importance of managing money. Save half and spend half (be responsible but also have fun and treat yourself). I first started the piggy bank tradition with Chad and you, Cliff... not anticipating that eventually there would be eight piggy banks to constantly feed with spare change. I enjoyed taking you kids, full piggy bank in hand, to the Young Americans Bank where your coins were counted. We made guesses on how much it would be... 40, 50, 80 dollars?

When we first opened your accounts, you had to stand on a step stool to look over the counter so you could watch the teller take care of your business, at the same time eyeing the jar with sweet treats on the counter... your reward for saving.

Children: Chad, Cliff, Carli and Thomas
Grandchildren: Irian, Max and Aelan (next page)

Back: Birgit with Chad and wife Tiffany
Front: Son in-law Zack with Carli and Thomas

Cliff, wife Yuri, Irian & Aelan

Thomas with son Max

Children: Heather, Shannon, Patricia and Trevor

Trevor, Patricia, Shannon, Heather, Heidi
and husband, Phil.

Epilogue

A grandchild's request…
"Omi, please come to my class
And tell us about the war
Was it scary?"

Daughters Birgit and Heidi said:
"Mutti, please write down your stories
As a gift to us and our children
And to their children"
And so it started…

I began writing in 2012
Stories about my family, the war, America
Digging deep into my memories
At times deeply cathartic… tears welling up
Writing for a non-writer is not easy…

Where to start, how to tell my stories,
How to make them interesting
To the reader
Not just narratives

Memoir writing classes helped me
Talented and experienced teachers
Patiently taught me to add detail, color and emotion
To my otherwise dry style
"How did it feel?" "What did it look like?"

"What color was the sky"
"Make your stories come alive through dialogue"

I learned so much and
Am still learning
I want to keep editing, editing, editing
Will it ever be done?
It took so long to get here
Almost ten years
Amazing how much I learned

About myself

I cannot express the joy I feel
Reflecting back
Now in my golden years

How blessed I am
How grateful I am.

Acknowledgements

This memoir would not have been possible without the help and support of many. My heartfelt appreciation and thanks go to:

My daughters Birgit and Heidi, who gave me those first nudges to write my stories, believing it would help shed light on our family history now and for generations to come.

Needing help with my writing skills, I enrolled in several memoir writing classes, most notably the Heart and Soul Writers' Workshop led by Kelly Jo Eldrege. Thank you Kelly, you taught me well.

Horst for his wonderful photography.

To the Denver Women's Press Club - I thank you for honoring me with second place in your 2014 Unknown Writers Contest for my story Child of War. This award by your esteemed organization was a tremendous confidence booster for me.

I was inspired by and thank my fellow writers Sue Hester, Hans Benes, Jean Rice and Frank Dance for their support and encouragement.

I thank my brother Willi Mannheim for his difficult task of translating part of this memoir into German.

Thank you Cliff Schonewill for the beautiful cover design.

A critical task in writing is proof-reading. I am grateful for the careful attention and expert advice from Chad Schonewill, Martin Sugg and Dr. Lowell Hansen.

Thank you to my eight grandchildren for their curiosity and thoughtful questions which added an important dimension to this work.

How fortunate was I that my daughter Birgit took on the role of editor and producer. She did so with never failing support and creativity. Thank you, Biggi, this couldn't have happened without you.

I thank my many friends and family members for lending an ear in this process.